Wildwater West Virginia

Volume I   The Northern Streams

Other Menasha Ridge Press Guidebooks

Wildwater West Virginia, Volume II, The Southern Streams, Paul Davidson and Ward Eister, with Dirk Davidson

Carolina Whitewater: A Canoeist's Guide to the Western Carolinas, Bob Benner

Appalachian Whitewater, Volume I, The Southern Mountains, Bob Sehlinger, Don Otey, Bob Benner, William Nealy, and Bob Lantz

Appalachian Whitewater, Volume II, The Central Mountains, Bill Kirby and Ed Grove

Northern Georgia Canoeing, Bob Sehlinger and Don Otey

Southern Georgia Canoeing, Bob Sehlinger and Don Otey

A Canoeing and Kayaking Guide to the Streams of Ohio, Volume I, Richard Combs and Stephen E. Gillen

A Canoeing and Kayaking Guide to the Streams of Ohio, Volume II, Richard Combs and Stephen E. Gillen

A Canoeing and Kayaking Guide to the Streams of Kentucky, Bob Sehlinger

A Canoeing and Kayaking Guide to the Streams of Tennessee, Volume I, Bob Sehlinger and Bob Lantz

A Canoeing and Kayaking Guide to the Streams of Tennessee, Volume II, Bob Sehlinger and Bob Lantz

A Canoeing and Kayaking Guide to the Streams of Florida, Volume I, North Central Peninsula and Panhandle, Elizabeth F. Carter and John L. Pearce

Whitewater Home Companion, Southeastern Rivers, Volume I, William Nealy

Whitewater Home Companion, Southeastern Rivers, Volume II, William Nealy

Kayaks to Hell, William Nealy

Whitewater Tales of Terror, William Nealy

Boat Builder's Manual, Charles Walbridge, editor

Shipwrecks: Diving the Graveyard of the Atlantic, Roderick Farb

Smoky Mountains Trout Fishing Guide, Don Kirk

A Fishing Guide to Kentucky's Major Lakes, Arthur B. Lander, Jr.

A Fishing Guide to the Streams of Kentucky, Arthur B. Lander, Jr.

A Guide to the Backpacking and Day-Hiking Trails of Kentucky, Arthur B. Lander, Jr.

A Guide to Kentucky Outdoors, Arthur B. Lander, Jr.

Wildwater
West Virginia

Volume I The Northern Streams

Paul Davidson, Ward Eister,
and Dirk Davidson

THIRD EDITION

Menasha Ridge Press   *Hillsborough, North Carolina*

Copyright © 1972, 1975 by Robert G. Burrell and Paul C. Davidson;
   © 1985 by Paul C. Davidson, Ward Eister, and Dirk Davidson
All rights reserved
Printed in the United States of America
Published by Menasha Ridge Press
   Hillsborough, North Carolina
ISBN 0-89732-021-2
Third Edition, First printing, 1985

Cover photograph of "Wonderful Waterfall" on the Big Sandy
   courtesy of Newton Logan. Cover design by Carolyn Healy.

Library of Congress Cataloging in Publication Data:
Davidson, Paul, 1931 Dec. 12–
   Wildwater West Virginia.

   Rev. ed. of: Wild water West Virginia / Bob Burrell. 1972
   Includes indexes.
   Contents: v. 1. The northern streams — v. 2. The southern streams.
   1. White-water canoeing— West Virginia—Guide-books
—Collected Works.   2. West Virginia—Description and travel
—1981–   —Guide-books—Collected works.
I. Eister, Ward, 1941–   . II. Davidson, Dirk, 1956–
III. Burrell, Robert.   Wild water West Virginia.
IV. Title: Wild water West Virginia.
GV776.W4D38   1985   917.54′044   85-7126
ISBN 0-89732-021-2 (pbk : v. 1)
ISBN 0-89732-029-8 (pbk : v. 2)

Menasha Ridge Press
Route 3, Box 450
Hillsborough, North Carolina 27278

Table of Contents

Chapter 3   Fastest Water to the North—The Tygart Sub-Basin

Chapter 4   The Northwest Quadrant—The Ohio Basin

Chapter 5   And a Couple from Neighboring States

Preface to the Third Edition

In 1961 I met Bob Burrell—the most talented, industrious, bull- (and bald-) headed bastard in the forest. In 1965 we started to canoe mountain rivers. No one we knew did it. The West Virginia natives considered it absolute folly. With no teachers we sacrificed multiple canoes to the river gods before the Czechoslovakian slalom canoe came to our attention. Henri DeMarne, John Berry, Dan Sullivan, John Sweet, and Jim Rawleigh came out of the East to our rescue. They pulled us off the rocks, put us in closed boats, and showed us the Cheat, Yough, New, and Gauley rivers. In 1969 (and again in 1972) we tried to repay these generous guides to whitewater by reporting on our homework; we assembled a paddler's guide to the rivers and streams of West Virginia.

This original guide, *A Canoeist's Guide to the Whitewater Rivers of West Virginia*, was financed by the West Virginia Wildwater Association. The five hundred copies of this typed book stimulated us to collect more West Virginia rivers. Walter Burmeister's monumental classic, *Appalachian Waters*, was our index to rivers and Randy Carter's *Rivers of Virginia and West Virginia* was our model.

Seeing limitations of veracity in other guides, we vowed to only report on rivers we had paddled, to cover all of a geographic area—the state of West Virginia—and to write only after multiple trips of a given section at various water levels. (Where we have fallen short on this last point, we have stated so.) Bob's drive and my obsession for recording observations were joined in the first editions of this book. The result was twofold. We achieved some notoriety among the rapidly growing numbers of paddlers, but we also attracted many paddlers to our secret mountain streams. Without the guidebook, the out-of-state paddlers might have stayed on a few congested rivers and the locals might have stuck to fishing.

Unfortunately, this influx of paddlers to West Virginia split our team. My position was that paddling was growing anyway and this book only served to dilute the crowd over more streams. Bob's position, however, was that we had done a disservice to the wilderness by advertising it too widely, and so, in 1974, Bob bowed out. Now, many years later, I think he had a point. Much of the wilderness aspect of whitewater has been lost. The commercial boaters have turned the old favorites into ribbons of flesh and neoprene. The boat rotors and thermoplastic benders have taken away the prerequisite of having to design and build one's own equipment. Lost is the pioneer quality of whitewater. I still contend that this guidebook can serve to dilute the hoards, but I say that with less certainty than I previously expressed.

Ward Eister is an old paddling buddy dating back to 1967. He was the mainstay of the West Virginia Wildwater Association newsletter and an avid trip reporter of the miscellany of West Virginia streams for thirteen years. With Bob Burrell uninterested and with me out of state, Ward was asked if he would help update and revise a new edition. He accepted the task with enthusiasm. Sifting through the remaining uncharted streams of the state, he located a few gems as well as the slugs when he looked under the coal industry's polluted rocks of southwestern West Virginia. Unfortunately, the economics of the eighties translocated Ward to California before the task could be completed, making the book again an orphan in its own home.

One of the prides of my paddling career is the interest and excellence my sons have demonstrated on rivers. When Ward left the state my son Dirk took up the blue pencil. He cleaned up our text, adding his own crisp and accurate slalom strokes when we tended to brace through some literary holes.

Special credit must be given to Ed Gertler for his outstanding and generous contributions of reports and data. Although not a resident of West Virginia, Ed has probably paddled more West Virginia streams than any other individual. His aid has been invaluable and we are grateful. Ed is the author of a guidebook, *Maryland and Delaware Canoe Trails* (available from Seneca Press, 503 Bonifant St., Silver Springs, MD 20910).

My very good friend and an outstanding editor, Kathleen Case, voluntarily advised me on the use of the English language as a medium for conveying information to paddlers.

Also I want to acknowledge and thank the multiple other persons who have come to my rescue, on or off the river, during these many years of being in love with rivers and mountains and this corner of the earth.

SYOR
PCD

Wildwater West Virginia

Volume I   The Northern Streams

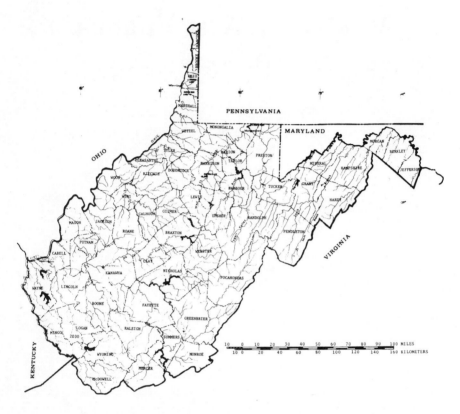

Map of West Virginia counties and primary streams.

From *Water Resources Data, West Virginia, Water Year 1983.*
U.S. Geological Survey WV-83-1, 1984.

Introduction

This guide is a collective effort of members of the West Virginia Wildwater Association who since 1965 have been paddling and exploring the creeks, streams, and rivers in almost every nook and cranny in the state by means of whitewater boats and techniques. Their efforts have been hampered by sparse numbers, poor roads, long drives, faulty maps, and vagaries of the weather, so it is with an exceeding sense of pride that these collected experiences are offered to the whitewater paddler at large and those interested in the West Virginia outdoors in general. More than an encyclopedia of mountain rivers and hydrologic data, it is a collection of experiences and memories, an introduction to some of the amazing geography of the Mountain State, and a plea for its preservation in a time when so many are unwisely ignoring and abusing these treasures.

Hundreds of miles of additional experience and exploration have enabled us to be more precise and thorough in this edition. The present guide is an attempt to be as comprehensive for the entire state as possible, perhaps an overly ambitious goal. Probably no one will ever run all of the whitewater in our state, but we feel that all of the significant water, and a good deal of the insignificant water, has been dealt with here.

Specific changes you will notice in this edition are the addition of many streams in the western part of the state, a region almost totally ignored in the first two editions. Also included are some smaller streams that offer avenues (alleyways?) of escape from the increasing numbers of paddlers on the more popular runs. Second reflections and error corrections have also created some minor changes.

While the use of the word *wild* in the first and second editions of *Wildwater West Virginia* suggests fast-flowing rivers, in this edition it connotes free-flowing wilderness rivers. Wild in the unbridled sense. We realize that pleasant pastoral surroundings may be as wild as we get in some parts of the state; there, the only thing wild is Saturday night at the local bar.

A number of things have changed in the last several years. The Cheat, New, and Gauley rivers have been victims of the burgeoning popularity of the sport, including the onslaught of commercial raft outfitters. In the summer months an estimated one hundred thousand people travel the New River, making it somewhat less than idyllic.

Though we are pleased, in some ways, with the growth of our "baby," we hope this growth will not be so great as to saturate the West Virginia wildwater out of existence. We would hate having to drop the word *wild* from our title.

This guidebook itself has also changed. It has evolved from a guide aimed at the intermediate paddler to one that offers something for everyone, from family camper to whitewater expert.

Included in the introduction are a few explanatory sections that both the seasoned paddler and the curious nonpaddler should read first. To begin with, the glossary sets the tone for the descriptions, to give you an idea of what to expect, and to get the housekeeping chores out of the way. We suggest you read this entire section in order to understand our specialized terms. Every subculture develops its own "lingo." It's imperative that you learn how to talk whitewater talk. Similarly, since the subject of river classification is so controversial, we have gone to great lengths to explain our values of river rating. This section should also be read before proceeding on to the main text. You will find a regional introduction at the start of each chapter concerning a particular system of rivers.

In most instances, the description of a section of a river is preceded by the following data: river miles of the section described, river classification, gradient, volume, type of scenery, time needed to travel, and water level. The descriptions are usually followed by information concerning difficulties, how to set up a shuttle, and the location of a gauge. However, some rivers and streams do not require as full a treatment as that, and we have accordingly omitted anything more than rudimentary data and a basic description.

Distance and Time. Each description gives the river miles traversed between put-in and take-out. We have given conservative paddling times for the runs we have clocked. These times do not include lunch, scouting, playing, or slothful behavior. Wind, flips, water level, and your ability may greatly alter the times listed. In general, figure on 3 mph. (Unless otherwise specified, right and left refer to directions as you look downstream.)

River Classification. Our river classification is based on the system devised by the American Whitewater Affiliation, although we prefer Arabic to their Roman numerals. (Please read our full discussion of classification in a separate introductory section below.)

Gradient. We have defined gradient as the average drop of the river in feet per mile (fpm). If parts of the river drop at a value significantly different from the average, we have given that additional information in parentheses. For example, 40(3@60) means that while the river drops an average of 40 fpm, 3 miles of it drop at 60 fpm.

Volume. Merely knowing the gradient, however, isn't enough. One must also consider the volume. A steep, high-volume river is generally much more difficult than a small stream of the same gradient. We have used as an index of volume the annual mean discharge in cubic feet per second (cfs), where 400 is the division between small (S) and medium (M) and 1500 the division between medium and large (L). Where the volume is significantly below 400, the letter designation is VS. If gauge data are available, numeric data are given in the text. If not, a letter designation of the volume indicates our best guess. As a rule of thumb, rivers are runnable when the flow equals or exceeds the value listed. They should be avoided during seasons when they are below this figure and approached with caution when they exceed a value three times their *average* discharge. The small rivers are early spring and very late fall runs. The larger rivers have a fall-winter-spring–season, but with dangerous midseason high levels. Often the government bureaus can give you the cfs flow of a particular river, and knowing the mean annual discharge of a river you are familiar with will help you in comparing it with a river new to you.

Level. Each river has its own personality when it comes to "too high" and "too low" and must be learned by experience. If two figures are listed under LEVEL, the first one is the lowest it has been run and the second is the highest (in our experience). If only one figure is listed, it indicates a minimum level needed to run a river. Where we've not been able to get a specific figure, we have listed the level as "NA," meaning not available. (In some cases, the level needed to run a river depends on seasonal rain or flooding, and so a specific figure has been omitted.) In general, our zeros are rather liberal as we do not enjoy scraping over rivers that are too low. Measuring the discharge of a river consists of measuring the cross-sectional area and flow velocity of the river over the full range of its levels at the gauging site. Since the most readily measurable of these related variables is the surface level, tables are compiled relating the discharge in cubic feet of water per second to depth measured in hundredths of feet. Where these gauges are convenient, we have used them to indicate runnable levels on each river section. At other places there are gauges painted on bridges and rocks by various paddlers. These boating gauges are done in the style of the late Randy Carter, the guidebook author who was our inspiration. On

Carter gauges, zero is the minimal paddling level in the maker's estimation. One advantage of the more exact government gauges is that the information is collected and recorded daily. One can determine the level of the rivers over a wide area by making a few key phone calls. You will find the pertinent phone numbers listed in our discussion of "River Gauges," which we urge you to read.

A river's personality also makes itself felt in the class and the continuity of its rapids. In the lower Smoke Hole there is only one Class 4 rapids. If you get through this, you may not necessarily be ready to run the North Branch of the Potomac where there is a continual succession of Class 3 or 4 rapids. The New, Cacapon, Greenbrier, and middle Yough all have widely spaced rapids, whereas Glady Fork, Seneca Creek, the Meadow, and the Savage contain one long continuous rapids each. Paddlers who are comfortable on the Cacapon will find the lower Glady Fork much more exciting, although the difficulty of the individual rapids is no greater.

Scenery. Scenery is ranked on an A to D scale:

A— remote, wilderness areas with little sign of civilization

B— more settled, but still beautiful pastoral countryside

C— a lot of development (cities or industry) or nothing scenically exciting

D— acid pollution, strip mines, tipples, slagheaps, gross pollution, povertyvilles, and other forms of ultimate landscape abuse

The quality of the scenery along a river can change quickly. For example, the Elk River below Sutton is usually considered B, even A at times, but immediately becomes D when it passes through Clay. Cities and man-made settings are not necessarily eyesores. Parsons, Philippi, Petersburg, and especially Harpers Ferry look pretty from the river. Morgantown, Richwood, and Webster Springs do not.

Directions. Finding your way around West Virginia is very difficult, and even the major attractions are poorly marked. We have included reproductions of maps from various sources near our descriptions of specific trip segments and shuttles. You will find the maps useful and even necessary for those regions where access points are especially hard to find. Hence this book should be carried in the car to help locate the put-ins and take-outs. (You should also have an additional copy in your pack, and since that one is likely to get wet, you should have a third copy at home.) Most of these sites can be reached by ordinary car providing there is no snow. A few are usable only by high-clearance, four-wheel-drive vehicles and are so indicated. Some roads are privately owned and permission to use them must be obtained beforehand. In a few cases, the river is not accessible by roads of any kind. Here the avid paddler will discover that his two lower appendages are not as useless as he had thought. (For more about maps, see the introductory section below on "Finding Your Way in West Virginia.")

To the person interested in the outdoors or the geography of West Virginia, let this guide show you the state as very few people see it and point out places of wonder that you didn't know existed. To the person who is fascinated by the sight and sound of moving water, let it be a lesson in applied hydrology. To shutterbugs everywhere, let it be a lure to provide you with subject matter for your film whether you are interested in action, natural beauty, or novel backgrounds for your nudes. Finally, to federal and state legislators, the U.S. Army Corps of Engineers, the purveyors of electric power, and anyone else who believes that our public rivers are their own personal property just waiting for exploitation for private profit, let it serve as a warning about the treasures they would destroy. Let this guide awaken in all citizens a quest for knowledge and an appreciation of West Virginia's magnificent rivers, so that they can help us repulse such river rapers. Above all, let this book be a catalog of descriptions of some of our best natural resources that have not been described anywhere from such a continuous, river-level viewpoint. If this book piques the curiosity of just one nonpaddler enough to cause that person to see what some of these treasures are and what is happening to them, it will be considered a success.

See you on the river!

Glossary

Whitewater paddling, like most any other activity, has its own lexicon of cant expressions. The following glossary is necessary for three reasons: (1) to explain to the whitewater paddler precisely what we mean by these terms, as usage tends to vary from region to region; (2) to explain to the nonpaddler the lingo of applied hydrology; and (3) to explain some words or meanings that may not be found elsewhere or even exist.

Descriptive Adjectives

Bad—depends on who is talking; refers to anything from Class 1 to Class 5. An expert regards Class 1 as bad and 5 as good, but with a novice it's vice versa.

Bodacious—a particularly expressive adjective borrowed from one of Appalachia's most celebrated heroes, Snuffy Smith. Used to describe anything in a truly superlative way.

Good—see *Bad*.

Horrendous—an adjective reserved for the most ferocious rapids. A cultured variant of "bodacious."

Juicy—a particularly heavy, aerated turbulence in which the C-1 boater gets hit in the chest and a K-1 in the face.

Hydrology and Hazards

Boulder Garden—a bodacious rock garden.

CFS—cubic feet per second; an accurate method of expressing river flow in terms of function of flow and volume.

Curler—a wave that curls or falls back on itself and you.

Doldrums—a pool without end.

Drop—an abrupt descent in the middle of a rapids.

Eddy—an area out of the mainstream. May be slowed, still, or reversed current. Downstream of an obstruction. Last name of a famous singer. Used by locals in eastern West Virginia to mean a pool.

Explosion Wave—a very violent and unpredictable wave.

Falls—a bodacious drop, although not necessarily straight down (a localism).

Gradient—the geographical drop of the river expressed in feet per mile (fpm).

Haystack—a high-standing wave caused by deceleration of current due to underwater resistance. Height of waves is measured from the trough to the crest. To get an idea of what the paddler experiences when getting ready to paddle a 7-foot wave, sit or kneel in front of a door and look up at the top of the jamb.

Hole or Souse Hole—the condition resulting from the turbulence created when fast water pours over a boulder which creates a depression of aerated turbulence immediately downstream of the boulder. The violent, downward hydraulic action of the water over the boulder often forces the stern downwards while the bow is forced upwards with equal violence on the turbulence, thus cracking the stern smartly. Will impede progress of boat. Paddlers must learn to escape a hole by paddling out the end or being swept out upside down. Learning these tricks converts many stoppers, keepers, and hydraulics into playing holes. In recent years these hazards have become the focus of thrill-seeking paddlers.

Hydraulic—similar to a souse hole but caused by water moving quickly over a low ledge or dam. Hydrologically, the two are very similar. The result may be the worst kind of keeper with a riverwide unbroken backwave.

Keeper—a bodacious stopper. A dangerous situation found in very heavy water which would be extremely difficult if not impossible to get out of if accidentally entered. A bad trip and something to be avoided.

Low-Water Bridge—a bridge made of multiple culverts and concrete that will be awash. Very dangerous for the paddler who, if not lodged in the culverts, may be trapped in the hydraulic.

Padded Boulder—see *Pillow*.

Pillow—a cushion of water on the upstream face of a rock or boulder. A "well-padded" boulder has a pillow that allows you to slide across the face of the rock without actually touching it. If the pillow is too thin, you get stuck on the upstream side of the rock.

Pool—flat water; no rapids.

Rapids—a collective noun referring to either a singular or plural set of waves, turbulences, etc., on a river. Like our pants and scissors, we do not use the word without a final *s*.

Riffle—a shallow rapids with very small waves.

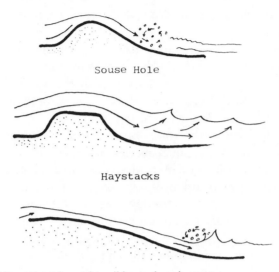

Souse Hole

Haystacks

Figure 1.   *Slide rapids with a curler and haystacks at bottom.*

Rock Garden—a rapids of Class 2 or 3 complexity characterized by many small, exposed or partially covered boulders that necessitate care in maneuvering.

Slide Rapids—an elongated ledge that descends or slopes gently rather than abruptly and is usually covered with only shallow water. Terminates in stopper-type waves.

Souse Hole—see *Hole*.

Stopper—any very heavy wave or turbulence that quickly impedes the downriver progress of a paddled boat.

Surfing Wave—a very wide wave that is fairly steep. Used for playing. A paddler can drive a boat upstream into it and stay balanced on its upstream face much in the same manner as a surfer on the face of an ocean wave.

Undercut Rock—a potentially dangerous situation in which a large boulder has been eroded or undercut by centuries of water flow. Could trap a paddler accidentally swept under it and pinned.

Personnel

Locals—natives of the area being paddled. They often have interesting ideas about the kind of people who are whitewater paddlers.

Skillful Paddlers—ourselves paddling a bodacious river.

Stupid Paddlers—others running a bodacious river without us.

U.S. Army Corps of Engineers—people who obtain drinking water from a full bathtub because they cannot stand the sight and sound of running water.

Apparatus

C-1—a completely *and* integrally decked whitewater canoe which looks like a kayak to the uninitiated.

C-2—same as C-1 but seating two persons. Such esoteric varieties as "slalom" or "wildwater" are beyond the scope of this glossary.

Deck—that part of the boat that covers the hull to prevent water from entering. Contains one or two cockpit openings for occupant(s).

K-1—a whitewater kayak that looks like a kayak even to the initiated.

Open Boat—loosely used by us to refer to any conventional canoe. When used on Class 4–5 water the paddler is by definition a macho-masochist.

Skirt—literally that; worn by paddler and fits snugly around waist at the top and around cockpit flange at the bottom to keep water from entering cockpit.

Technique

Bagel—a flip followed by a swim.

Brace—basic paddling technique used most often to prevent a boat from flipping in unstable situations. Exists in several varieties: high, low, inadequate.

Broach—to be turned broadside to the current; a no-no.

Draw—basic paddling technique of moving boat sideways toward the paddle.

Eddy Out—one of the few ways a paddler has to stop in the middle of a rapids. Enter an eddy or area of differential current by turning 180 degrees and pointing upstream. Very spectacular, particularly when attempted and failed just upstream from a juicy drop.

Ender—an end-over-end roll. Usually done by design and with effort, skill, and luck by paddling upstream on a surfing wave or into a hydraulic. The bow is pushed down and under, the paddler falls on his head, the cameras whir and click, ladies swoon, the paddler rolls up, and all yahoo.

Flip—upset; wipe out; turn over; bottom up.

Paddling by the Seat of Your Pants—paddling a river without any prior knowledge of it and without scouting.

Pinned—helplessly snagged or caught in a rapids by a forceful current pressing the boat and/or paddler against an immovable object. Made worse if paddler is pinned between the boat and the object. Made much worse if paddler is folded inside the pinned boat. A very dangerous situation.

Pop-up—an aborted ender.

Pry—opposite of draw.

Roll—saving face after a flip by using a well-practiced paddle stroke when upside down that enables boat to be returned right side up with occupant still in place. Should be required skill of any paddler on Class 4 water.

Scout—to carefully examine a rapids before running it. The way to run a complex rapids may not be readily obvious.

Shuttle—since it is impractical to paddle back up the river you have just descended, most paddling parties arrange to have a car(s) or other means of transportation at the take-out point and then drive other cars to the put-in. Often takes hours and is referred to as "setting up the shuttle." Shuttling is an art frequently foiled by lost car keys, flat tires, missed road signs, knocked-out oil pans, inept shuttlers, and forgetting a copy of *Wildwater West Virginia*.

Sneak—to take a less formidable route around a difficult spot.

Snuck—past tense of sneak.

Take the Girl Scout Route—see *Sneak*.

Miscellaneous Expressions

See You on the River—traditional sign-off used by whitewater paddlers in place of such trite expressions as good-bye, so long, be seein' you, toodle-oo. Abbreviated SYOR.

Y'er Crazier 'en Hell—frequent expression of locals observing whitewater paddlers splash by.

Whitewater Difficulty Rating System

The rating of whitewater seems to be a very controversial subject, and the debate over what class a particular rapids is goes on and on. The most dangerous river ratings are from the truly expert paddler who either has forgotten what it was like to be ordinary or perhaps never even knew. Such folk tend to underrate everything. On the other hand, the inexperienced paddler goes too far the other way and tends to overrate everything. What seems horrendous to him (and rightly so) may only be a Class 3.

To settle such arguments, two solutions come to mind. One is to have a standard paddler run all of the rivers. This is what we have done, using ourselves as the standard. The other solution is to use an objective point system and let the chips fall where they may. This we have tried to do to confirm our impressions by following the guidelines set by the American Whitewater Affiliation. Certain key characteristics which shouldn't lead to any arguments are assigned point values, and all of these are totaled up. The final score determines the class.

We have tried to strictly define each class and stick to these definitions in rating each river. We have also observed that a river can be approximately classified by multiplying the logarithm of the gradient in fpm by the logarithm of the flow in cfs and subtracting 1—e.g., 1,000 cfs and 100 fpm; (log 1,000 $\times$ log 100) – 1; (3 $\times$ 2) – 1 = 5. Like any system of classification, it is a human attempt to sort out disorder and, being a human activity, is subject to human foibles.

Flat Water

Class A—Standing or slow-flowing water, not more than 2.5 mph.

Class B—Current between 2.5 and 4.5 mph, but backpaddling can effectively neutralize the speed.

Class C—Current more than 4.5 mph. Backpaddling cannot neutralize the speed of the current. Simple obstacles may occur that require a certain amount of boat control.

Whitewater

Class 1—Easy. Occasional small riffles consisting of low, regular wave patterns. About what you might encounter on a lake on a mildly windy day. Most of the Elk River below Sutton or the Cheat River between Parsons and Rowlesburg.

Class 2—Medium difficulty. Rapids occur more frequently, usually retaining a regular wave pattern as on a lake with a fairly vigorous wind (enough to cause whitecaps). Although there may be more than one route, the most practical one is easily determined. There may be simple, uncomplicated chutes over ledges up to 3 feet high. Almost all of Shavers Fork north of US 33.

Class 3—Difficult. Numerous rapids, with higher, irregular-standing waves, hydraulics, and eddies. The main thing about Class 3 is that you are forced to maneuver in the rapids. The most practical route is not always obvious, and you'll find that you start having to work a little. Ledges up to 4 feet, waves up to 3 feet, overhanging branches, and deeper water characterize this class. The Hopeville Canyon of the North Fork (South Branch of the Potomac) at medium- to high-water levels and the Quinnimont Rapids of the New River.

Class 4—Very difficult. Long, extensive stretches of rapids with high, irregular standing waves and difficult hydraulics, holes, eddies, and crosscurrents. Decks are desirable, as is a high degree of boat control. Not only are you working, but you are working very hard. Class 4 requires a good deal of instant decisions because the most practical route is not obvious. Difficult ledges with irregular passages, "stopper" waves, or souse holes in the way. This class includes most of the really difficult water in the state and covers a lot of ground technically. The Cheat Canyon at medium levels, the North Branch of the Potomac at low to medium, and a lot of the Tygart River are solidly in this class.

Class 5—Exceedingly difficult. This is a hard class to define; it's difficult to tell where Class 4 ends and 5 begins. There is very little Class 5 in the state at normal levels, although many rivers can take on this character in high water. The rapids are not only difficult, but they are long and continuous. Irregular stoppers and souse holes are unavoidable, and partially submerged boulders and ledges are everywhere; very complex eddies and crosscurrents, etc., are not only present but also occur in long dazzling combinations. Common usage also refers to any single, dangerous rapids that requires a lot of skill and courage to run as Class 5, even if a short one. The Gauley River below Summersville Reservoir contains a good deal of this kind of water; the Double Z and certain others in the New River Gorge and a few on the Tygart are legitimate 5s.

Class 6—Utmost difficulty. This isn't a hard class to define, but in recent years there has been a tendency to ignore the definition. It is supposed to mean the utmost limit of navigability, and its chief distinguishing characteristic is *risk of life*. There has been a tendency to degrade any Class 6 rapids to a 5 once it has been run, but such practice is not followed in this guide. Flooded rivers often get up into this category. A mistake can be costly, and no one should ever be urged or taunted into running a 6 (or anything else for that matter).

When the difficulty of a river falls between two grades, two numbers are used, i.e., Class 2–3. If most of the river is of one classification except for one or two spots, it is referred to as, say, Class 3_4. Ratings used in this manual are for normal water levels. It should be kept in mind that these ratings might change drastically in high water. Similarly, if you run one of our Class 4s in very low water, don't think you are a Class 4 paddler. Ratings usually drop at least a class under such conditions.

Rapid below the bridge at Audra, Middle Fork
of the Tygart River

Photograph by Ward Eister

River Gauges

The water flow on most rivers in this country is quantified at frequent intervals by the Water Resources Division of the Geological Survey, Department of Interior. The data are recorded as discharge in cubic feet per second (cfs) and available to everyone. The principle is based on the velocity of flow past a point of known cross-sectional area in the river. Discharge is readily related to a single variable: the height of the river at a fixed point. Gauge houses, situated on most rivers, consist of a well at the river's edge with a float attached to a recording clock. The gauge reading is in hundredths of feet. Rating tables are constructed for each gauge relating these readings to discharge. The recorded gauge heights are collected regularly.

Some key geological survey gauges are reported to the Corps of Engineers and the National Weather Service offices very frequently for flood control and river navigational regulation. Power companies also need this information in operating hydroelectric dams. Some of these gauges are read by observers who call central offices at regular intervals. Some are attached to a telephone and can be read by a sound code, and a few are read by radio signal. Some gauges have data collected by messengers only at infrequent intervals.

The paddler can plan trips using this information. Most key gauge results can be obtained from offices dealing with an entire river basin:

- For gauges in the Potomac basin, call the National Weather Service in Maryland at (301) 899-7378 for a taped message available 24 hours a day. Gauge readings include those for Front Royal, Hancock, Kitzmiller, Petersburg, and Springfield.

- For gauges in the Monongahela basin (including the Cheat, the Tygart, and the Yough), call the National Weather Service in Pittsburgh at (412) 644-2890. A person answers the phone between 8:30 a.m. and noon; from noon on, a taped message provides gauge readings. Gauge readings include those for Belington, Buckhannon, Confluence, Friendsville, Markleton, Parsons, and Philippi.

- For gauges in the Kanawha basin (from the Greenbrier westward), call the Corps of Engineers in Huntington at (304)

529-5604. The phone is answered only on weekdays from
7:00 a.m. to 4:00 p.m. Kanawha basin gauge readings are
also available from the Hydrology Section of the National
Weather Service in Charleston at (304) 342-7771, Monday
through Friday, 8:00 a.m. to 4:30 p.m. Gauge readings include those for Alderson, Ashford, Belva, Branchland, Buck-
eye, Craigsville, Hinton, Mt. Lookout, Summersville, and
Webster Springs.

We also have phone numbers for some specific gauges:

- Potomac Basin
  A reading of the Capon Bridge gauge for the Cacapon is
  available from the Coryell Market in Capon Bridge; call
  (304) 856-2750.

- Monongahela Basin
  A reading of the Albright gauge for the Cheat Canyon is
  available from Morgan's Gas Station in Albright; call (304)
  329-1748.

- Kanawha Basin
  The Corps of Engineers at Summersville Dam provides
  readings of the Mt. Lookout gauge for the Meadow and the
  Summersville gauge for the Gauley; call (304) 872-5809.
  The Corps of Engineers at Bluestone Dam provides readings of the Pipestem gauge for the Bluestone and the Hinton
  gauge for the New; call (304) 466-1234 to get readings from
  an official of the Corps, or call (304) 466-0156 for a taped
  message.
  A reading of the Webster Springs gauge for the Elk and the
  Birch can be obtained by calling (304) 847-5532. This is
  a telemetering gauge; see our comments below about such
  devices.
  A reading of the Marlinton gauge for the Greenbrier is
  available from Brill's Exxon Station; call (304) 799-8229.

While gauge readings for the Potomac and Monongahela basins are
available round the clock, you can only get most gauge readings for the
Kanawha basin during business hours. We very much hope the Huntington and Charleston offices will soon provide a recorded message
listing gauge readings so paddlers can get the latest information at any

time of day and over weekends. This information should be made available as a news release comparable to skiing condition reports.

The Corps gets many of its gauge readings from gauges connected to the telephone system, but the phone numbers of these gauges are unlisted. Telemetering gauges send signals in a series of buzzes for tens, units, tenths, and hundredths, with an interval following each digit. Zeroes are a long buzz. An example for a 4.32-foot reading would be as follows: ——(0) ---- (4) --- (3) -- (2). Anyone calling such a gauge should realize that it is probably battery operated and that heavy use will prompt the Corps to change the phone number.

Jim Snyder surfing on the Tygart River

Photograph courtesy of C. M. Laffey, Appalachian Wildwaters

Finding Your Way in West Virginia

Trying to find take-outs and put-ins in whitewater country can be difficult unless you are native to the immediate area. Often topographical maps are quite helpful especially for geographical features. However, a good deal of West Virginia has not been surveyed for over 60 years (particularly those portions with the best whitewater) and landmarks such as railroads, bridges, and secondary roads have changed somewhat since those days. Usually, however, they are helpful and in most cases, our river write-ups contain the quadrangle name for pertinent maps of the area. Unless stated otherwise, the quadrangle name is for the 7.5-minute size. Larger, 1:125,000 scale maps are also available; a set of 9 covers the state. These maps may be obtained from the West Virginia Geological Survey, Room 2, White Hall, West Virginia University Campus, Morgantown, WV 26506, and from various other locations throughout the state.

A very good map to have is the Monongahela National Forest map (MNF). This map contains the best features of road maps and topo maps. It is very good and up to date for finding the remoter put-ins for rivers in the forest or in lands contiguous with it. It is also quite helpful for places of natural interest, hiking, trails, and camping sites. National forest maps are obtainable from any district ranger's office or by writing the Forest Supervisor, Monongahela National Forest, Elkins, WV 26241.

The official state road map is practically worthless in that secondary roads are not numbered and many important shuttle roads are not even on it. It is good for finding locations of state parks and major highways.

County road maps are excellent, especially in finding secondary roads; however, private and forest service roads are not always on them. Prices of the county road maps vary according to the map size ordered. Sets are available either loose leaf or bound. To get these maps, write for a free price list from the West Virginia Department of Highways, Advanced Planning Division, Charleston, WV 25311.

Under SHUTTLE directions for each river, a federal highway is prefixed with US as in US 220, a major state highway with WV as in WV 39, forest service roads with FS as in FS 92, while state secondary and tertiary roads (county roads in most states) with CR as in CR 6 or they may appear in quotes as in "6". Strangers may have a hard time finding road signs with this number. At most intersections you will find a green sign (often with bullet holes) naming the county and followed by an encircled number, e.g., Preston ⑥. This doesn't mean that it is 6 miles to Preston. Six is the number of the secondary road.

Maps used as illustrations in this book are primarily topographical maps, or the Monongahela National Forest map (MNF). Scales are given whenever we change from one type of map to another.

1 George Washington's River and Its Tributaries— The Potomac Drainage

Of all the rivers in the state, the mighty Potomac and its tributaries are by far the most historic. Sometimes referred to as George Washington's River or the Nation's River, the Potomac has witnessed and has been a part of our country's birth and growth. Much of the upper drainage remains nearly the same as it was in George's day. It is a huge and fascinating watershed of outstanding beauty that offers an almost un-limited variety of whitewater adventure. This is truly canoe and kayak country at its best.

As will be pointed out frequently, most of the headwaters of the Potomac, especially the Cacapon and the South Branch tributaries, are characterized by immense cliffs and rock formations which provide some of the most breathtaking scenery in West Virginia. Caudy's Castle, Royal Glen or Petersburg Gap, Seneca, Eagle, and Champe Rocks are, of course, known well enough to have their own names, but there aren't enough names in the book to give to all of such formations, many of which can only be seen by the whitewater paddler. The lime-stone sedimentary layers of the South Branch highlands have been eroded by underground rivers for centuries, creating underground a spelunker's bonanza with caves of as much variety, beauty, and chal-lenge as that offered to the paddlers and rock climbers aboveground. Smoke Hole and Seneca Caverns are, of course, well known to the public, but Cave Mountain, Schoolhouse, Hell Hole, and the like are examples of caves known intimately only by the skilled spelunker. Few areas in the country can boast that they look as good underground as above.

The main stem of the Potomac is formed near Green Spring by its 2 major branches—the beautiful, bountiful water of the South Branch, most of which arises in the mountains of Highland County, Virginia, and the ugly, polluted water of the North Branch which arises at Lord Fairfax's survey stone where the extreme southwestern tip of Maryland cuts down into West Virginia's Eastern Panhandle. Later, near Berkeley Springs, the Potomac picks up the Cacapon system and then a little farther merges with the Shenandoah to form West Virginia's eastern-most tip, Harpers Ferry.

The North Branch never gets a chance to be beautiful. It starts right in the midst of some of the worst air pollution and strip mining in the country and never really sees anything much better. The water, laden with silt and mine acids, passes through the most depraved communities imaginable, where tossing garbage in the river is not only a habit but a way of life. It then flows into a reservoir designed to assure low-water augmentation as it continues on to receive the discharges from paper mills, factories, and municipal sewage plants. Some of the scenery is pretty and even quite striking, but too often it is pretty depressing, like that at Shallmar, Maryland—a long row of unpainted houses, in front of which the river bank is fouled continuously by garbage and refuse, and behind which are the most devastating ravages of strip mining anywhere. As Charles Morrison has written, "Some scars of . . . early industrialization are still to be found along the North Branch. And today, the by-products of modern industry—air and water pollution and defacement of the land—are more evident along the North Branch than anywhere else in the valleys of the Potomac. But there is a danger in other parts of the Valley as well. Either we cherish this 'Cradle of the Republic' as Gutheim called it, or we let it become stifled by the refuse of unplanned and uncontrolled exploitation."

The South Branch can be thought of as the collection of 3 main tributaries—the South Branch proper, the North Fork, and the South Fork or Moorefield River. The distance separating the 2 streams farthest from each other at potential put-ins (Circleville and Fort Seybert) is but 17 miles. Each of these rests in its own beautiful valley separated from its neighbor only by a single high mountain ridge. All of them begin as clear, cold trout streams, gradually drawing warmth from the fabulous South Branch valley, until they reach the area below Petersburg and Moorefield, where they mingle to form some of the finest warm-water fishing in the eastern United States. Seneca Creek, Little Cacapon, Patterson Creek, New Creek, and North River are significant minor tributaries in the magnificent basin.

Since all of the early explorations of this area followed the rivers, the Potomac tributaries are laden with history. The early settlers traced these valleys in their quest for freedom and independence. The rivers were the main channels of transportation for people and goods from the beginning until very recent times. In addition, as elsewhere throughout the state, the railroads usually followed the river valleys. Finally, political boundaries were drawn either at the rivers themselves or at the edge of their watersheds. George Washington was the most celebrated of the early explorers of the Potomac valleys. His aim was to find a means to connect the Potomac and Ohio River basins by waterways. He did not succeed, but what he learned in his travels and recorded in his journals influenced subsequent events in these lands.

Little of the French and Indian and Revolutionary wars actually penetrated the Potomac Highlands due to the transportation difficulties, but a few sites are memorable. Chief among these is Old Fields, just north of Moorefield near the head of the Trough. The Indians first burned away the forest here to form fields. Later one of the first white settlements was made here only to be annihilated in 1756 in an Indian battle. Old Fields later became an important stop on various transportation routes, situated as it was on the South Branch and also at the intersection of the Seneca Trail and McCullough's Path, 2 of West Virginia's earliest highways. Several defense forts of the West Virginia frontier were located in this area. In addition to Fort Pleasant at Old Fields, there were some 30 others, 2 of which, Fort Ashby and Fort Seybert, still exist in whitewater country. Terrible Indian massacres led by Killbuck and his warriors occurred within 24 hours of each other at this latter fort and at Upper Tract.

The Potomac headwaters witnessed much of the Civil War, although no major battle like that at Antietam Creek was fought here. Sectionalism literally tore the highlands apart, politically as well as militarily. The Potomac Highlands escaped with only "minor" skirmishes; Romney, for example, changed hands some 56 times, and there were wild chases through Franklin and at Old Fields. Fort Mulligan, located high above the river just west of Petersburg, was occupied by northern troops, and the trenches and gun emplacements are still visible, as is a water tank of more recent vintage squarely within the outline of the fort. Keyser, then called New Creek (they should have left it like that), was an important outpost, as was Moorefield. Saltpeter was mined in Cave Mountain in the Smoke Hole. But of course when one thinks of the Civil War, one thinks of Harpers Ferry where the whole shootin' match started. A National Park Service park now commemorates and displays some of the original buildings and fortifications of Harpers Ferry near the mouth of the Shenandoah (try this for an interesting lunch stop). Moorefield also keeps some of this heritage alive when each year in late September many of the antebellum homes in the area are opened for public display.

Several parks exist in the area for camping or touring, but few of these are on or near rivers. Suitable developed spots for camping in conjunction with paddling are the Forest Service campgrounds at Seneca Creek, Smoke Hole, and Big Bend, but there are no other suitable campgrounds on the rivers. All of the land is either privately owned or inaccessible. Some of the landowners will give camping permission (some for a small fee), but their lands are all underdeveloped and without sanitary facilities.

Potomac streams are known throughout the East for fine bass and trout fishing. Suckers, muskies, and fallfish are very common, as are bluegills and redeyes. The Shenandoah is well known for its different species of catfish. All of the lower Potomac and the Cacapon also produce eels. The forest communities and the prevalence of pulpwood production on family farms help sustain the large populations of deer and wild turkey. Hunter success is very high for these species as well as for the large numbers of squirrels that live in the abundant oak forests. The black bear finds refuge in the very high, isolated areas, such as North Fork Mountain, but it would be highly unlikely for a paddler to see one. Beaver and muskrats are common, especially along the Moorefield and Cacapon rivers, but being close to the Atlantic flyway, it is the variety and numbers of waterfowl that are the most impressive. The shale barrens of the Panhandle are associated with some unusual plant communities, perhaps the most unique member of which is the prickly pear cactus, a plant well adapted to the summer droughts common to this area. The Panhandle is well known for its apple orchards, grazing, and poultry production. The farms are well kept, productive, and attractive.

Few dams exist in the area. Among the most interesting are those that are built below Cumberland on the Potomac for maintenance of the famous Chesapeake and Ohio Canal. Begun in 1828 and completed in 1850, the system consisted of 74 locks which had to lift or lower a mule-drawn barge a collective total of 605 feet. The barges moved only about 2 mph or slower than a C-1 against the wind and were a very noncompetitive but leisurely form of transportation. Such traffic existed until 1924, and many of these dams still impound water. There are a few power company dams around—one on the Shenandoah above Millville, one on the Potomac below Williamsport, one on the Stony River headwaters, and one on the Cacapon down near its mouth. There are a couple of dams in the vicinity of Cumberland, but nobody in his right mind paddles the North Branch near there. Pumped storage projects are becoming more popular, and the kilowatt-hour people are vying with the Corps for the choice sites. The Corps' activities have been confined to building a dam on the North Branch below Shaw and pushing hard to build one at lovely Royal Glen above Petersburg.

NORTH BRANCH OF THE POTOMAC RIVER

A. Henry to Gormania—8 Miles

CLASS	GRADIENT	VOLUME	SCENERY	TIME	LEVEL
1–2$_4$	40	159	D	2	5–7'

MAPS: USGS—Kempton, Table Rock, and Gorman
       COUNTY—Grant

DESCRIPTION: This run starts in the shadow of Fairfax Stone, the historic survey mark dividing Maryland and The Old Dominion and indicating the headwaters of the Potomac. This section is an easy run with only 1 good whitewater section about 1 mile below Wilson. Look for a 6-foot slide.

SHUTTLE: WV 90 parallels the run.

GAUGE: The Kitzmiller gauge is 13 miles downstream. It must be unusually high for this little headwater run. Call (301) 899-3210 for a reading.

B. Steyer, Maryland to Kitzmiller, Maryland—13 Miles

CLASS	GRADIENT	VOLUME	SCENERY	TIME	LEVEL
3–4	51	159	A–D	4	4.5–6'

MAPS: USGS—Gorman, Mount Storm, and Kitzmiller
       COUNTIES—Grant and Mineral (a Maryland road map
             would also be helpful)

DESCRIPTION: Whoopee! This stream is probably the longest and most continuous difficult run in this part of the country. It descends rather steeply for its size, which accounts for the constant rapids, turbulence, and excellent action. The water isn't much to look at. It is polluted with mine acids and is usually muddy from the surrounding strip mines, but the scenery is mostly beautiful until you reach the garbage-laden banks, unpainted houses, and barren strip mines near Kitzmiller.

This is also the ledgiest river you will ever encounter and there must be at least a thousand hydraulics. The first mile below Steyer is a very

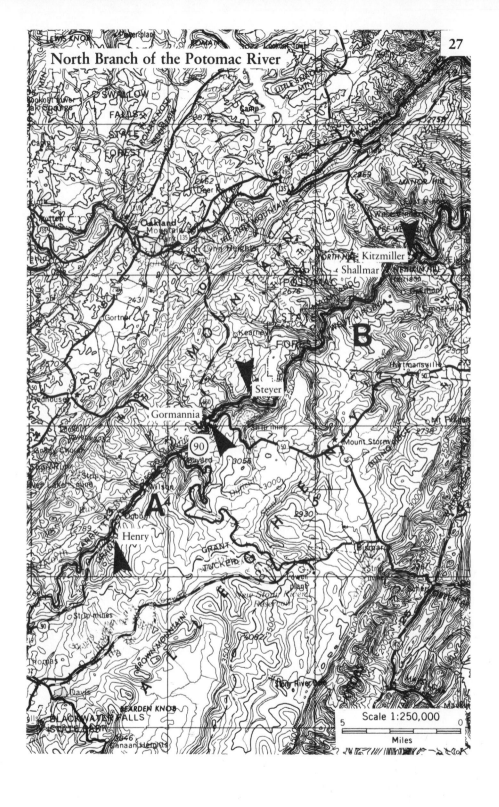

North Branch of the Potomac River

Scale 1:250,000

Miles

peaceful descent over Class 1–2 rapids. Then, every once in a while, a rather juicy drop through a narrow channel dampens your navel until, without much other warning, you are into it up to your eyeballs, and you realize that the gradient is really picking up. Almost all of the rapids have at least 1 ledge, usually made more complicated by sinister turbulences. It is very narrow and rocky all the way to the mouth of the Stony, where the volume of the river usually doubles.

Below the railroad bridge a half mile beyond the mouth of the Stony is the first of a series of really big drops. After this the river broadens out into an almost continuous series of haystack-filled rapids that do not require much maneuvering. You will appreciate this if you have just come down the Stony. However, this doesn't last long as the river narrows once again and the rapids become more difficult. Maneuvering becomes more necessary and the descents become powerful. Padded boulders, powerful souse holes, and difficult crosscurrents add spice to the run. This continues mile after mile. Rarely encountered is a stretch of quiet water longer than 50 yards.

DIFFICULTIES: Run the first island below Steyer on the right; it contains a nice drop into a hole. The second island has a mean passage on the left consisting of the old sharp-left-hand-drop-into-a-vicious-curler-hole-combination-out-into-another-hydraulic trick! At least one other group refers to this as Corkscrew Ledge. Fitting. From here on to the mouth of the Stony, the river is steep and mean. In high water, you will really be pushed around.

There are 4 ledges below the railroad bridge mentioned above. They are all within a distance of a half mile. The first 2 and the fourth are big drops into very heavy turbulence. The first is run on the left; it is the steepest and most complicated. Likewise, the second ledge is run on the left but it is much easier. You just drop down into the meringue. The third is obvious, but to run the fourth, you must get way over on the right. At 7 feet, a very dangerous level, some of these form *absolute keepers* and cannot be run. There is a pool between each for rescue purposes, at least at lower levels. About three-fourths of the way to Kitzmiller are the remains of some old concrete bridge abutments. The one on the left has toppled over, thus creating a dam in the main channel. Be careful, as the main force of the current smashes furiously against it. It can be run on the left or, at higher levels, snuck on the right.

The whole run is difficult. It is long and strenuous. You will be working every minute. This is not a good river to test out intermediates because there are no midway take-outs, only a long walk along the railroad tracks. Each paddler in the party should be competent and capable of taking care of himself. Much harder than the lower Yough.

SHUTTLE: The put-in can be reached from US 50 at Gormania by taking a dirt road down the Maryland side of the river for 2 miles to Steyer. A put-in can also be made on the Stony River at the US 50 bridge (see separate description). Take out at the bridge at Kitzmiller, Maryland, on MD 38 (reached from MD 135 between Oakland and Bloomington, Maryland) or from WV 42 via Elk Garden from US 50. To save 2 miles of comparatively less active water at the end, arrange a take-out at the godforsaken community of Shallmar, Maryland, just upstream from Kitzmiller.

GAUGE: Located at Kitzmiller. A painted gauge on the Maryland-side bridge pier corresponds to the telemetering gauge.

STONY RIVER

A. VEPCO Dam to US 50—7.6 Miles

CLASS	GRADIENT	VOLUME	SCENERY	TIME	LEVEL
2–4	71	83	A	3	4–6′

MAPS: USGS—Mount Storm Lake, Gorman, and Mount Storm
      COUNTY—Grant

DESCRIPTION: A small stream by creek standards, much less by river standards. Flow depends on releases by the VEPCO dam at Mount Storm. The river starts in a fairly easy manner but picks up to Class 4 in the middle of the run with the rapids becoming steep, boulder strewn, and often blind. Gradient evens out and rapids become longer and less severe toward US 50.

DIFFICULTIES: Precise boat control is needed in many of the steeper, more congested rapids. Also the small size of this stream dictates cautious observation for fallen trees.

SHUTTLE: Take out at US 50 bridge. Take the road to Bismarck "50/3" leading from the bridge and drive to WV 93. Turn right and drive to the sluice at the VEPCO dam. It is a long, steep carry from the road down to the put-in along the right side of the sluice. Put in on the pool below the turbulence.

GAUGE: See section B, below.

B. US 50 to North Branch of the Potomac—6 Miles

CLASS	GRADIENT	VOLUME	SCENERY	TIME	LEVEL
3–4	76	83	A	2	4–6′

MAPS: USGS—Mount Storm and Kitzmiller
      COUNTIES—Grant and Mineral

DESCRIPTION: The Stony, the Cheat, and the Savage are all well named, but this one especially so. Beginning placidly at the US 50 bridge, this little brawler begins to head downhill fast. Not only is the gradient steep throughout with hardly any slack water, but also the

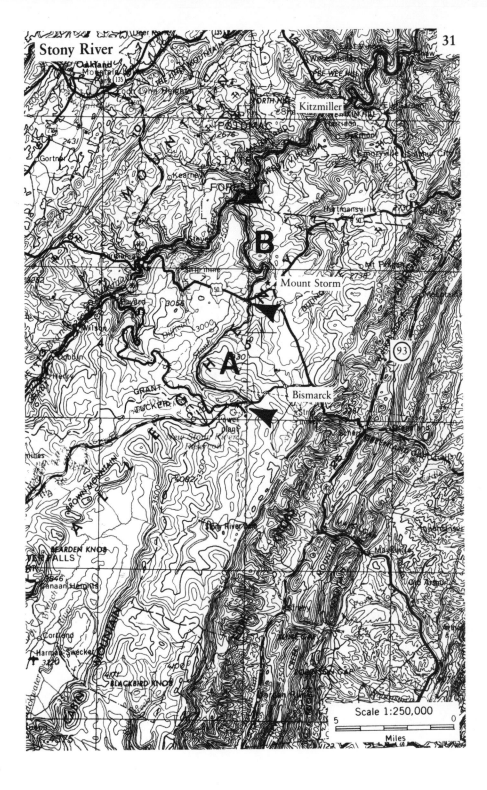

maneuvering around boulders, over ledges, and through complicated drops is extremely difficult and physically taxing. At low water the maneuvering is extreme and makes for the most challenging run. High water makes the maneuvering easier, but the drops and turbulence are more significant. At low levels this section is "easier" than the upper section, but it becomes harder in high water.

The flow can be controlled by the power company dam, but runs are limited to high water run-off periods in winter and spring. The scenery is pleasant woods, high cliffs, and picturesque falls, but located too close by are strip mines, coal piles, mine dumps, and similar crud. The water is clear, but polluted with mine acids.

DIFFICULTIES: The whole cotton-picking run is difficult. The Class 4 designation relates more to constant, intricate maneuvering in low water, but it can be up to Class 5 due to the heaviness at higher levels. Singling out any one particular rapids as worse than the others is impractical with the exception of the last big drop at the sawmill just one-quarter mile upstream from the mouth. This is a 6'+ waterfall which should be scouted. Mining and timbering activity have pushed numerous trees into the river, creating a particular hazard. This has, in fact, led to the death of one kayaker.

SHUTTLE: Put in under US 50 bridge. A take-out can be reached by turning north on the "Kuhn Mine Road" just east of Mount Storm. This hard road eventually splits. Keep to the left to avoid ending up in a strip mine. The last mile of road is bad for low-clearance vehicles. Take out just above the falls and the bridge. However, combining this trip with a run on the best part of the North Branch and taking out in Kitzmiller, Maryland, 2 hours and 9 miles downstream, is recommended. See separate description, section B of North Branch of the Potomac.

GAUGE: Located on left side, downstream from the Kitzmiller bridge. The lower levels are going to be scrapers.

ABRAM CREEK

US 50 to North Branch of the Potomac—8.5 Miles

CLASS	GRADIENT	VOLUME	SCENERY	TIME	LEVEL
2–4	47(1@110)	60	A–D	3	5.9'

MAPS: USGS—Kitzmiller and Mount Storm
COUNTIES—Mineral and Grant

DESCRIPTION: This is an exciting little stream. It is difficult to catch up and when it is, so is everything else. It starts off with a big, big bang right below US 50 and drops the 110 fpm. There are no big drops, but it is full of boulders for the first mile. It is steep, and of course much maneuvering is required. Most of the middle section is just fun-type riffles and open rapids of up to Class 3 difficulty which offer no particular difficulty. In fact, most of the river is that way. In the last mile there is not much maneuvering around boulders and the like, but there are big waves and complex currents, much like the Savage at 1,000 cfs (at least at the 5.9-foot level). The scenery alternates between pleasant woods and coal mines, haul roads, railroad tracks, and old houses.

DIFFICULTIES: The first mile is the hardest part and would compare with such streams as the upper Yough and the Stony. The easy middle section contains a low-water bridge which must be portaged, and since the bridge is in the middle of a rapids, it is best to carry the rapids. Toward the end, watch for a coal mine on the left bank. One or 2 rapids below this there is a big sliding ledge. It is advisable to scout this.

SHUTTLE: Put in at the US 50 bridge east of Mount Storm. To allow preview of the creek and gauge on the way to the take-out, go east on US 50 for 3 miles, turn left to Emoryville, and follow the creek through Oakmont to a railroad fork at the mouth.

GAUGE: The 5.9-foot reading refers to a government gauge located on the third bridge below the put-in, which is the second crossing after the left to Emoryville, but it is not conveniently located for inspection. The water at the 5.9-foot run was at the top of the base of the concrete abutment at US 50, an unlikely occurrence more than once a year. Inspection here and at the mouth should be satisfactory.

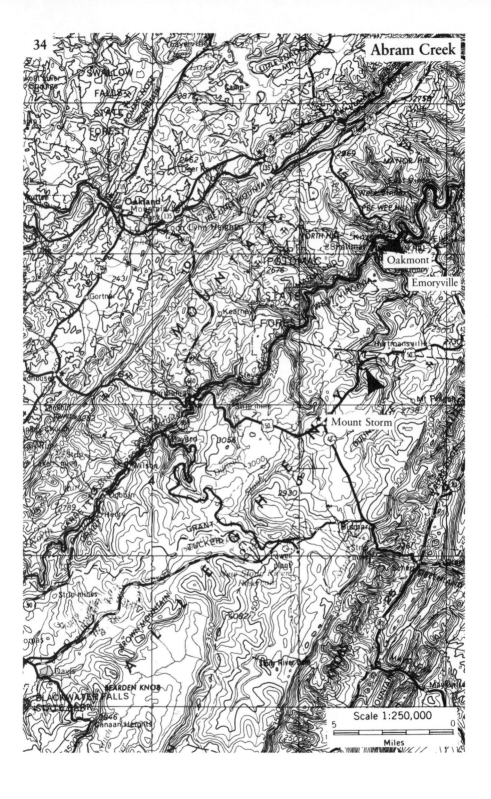

Abram Creek

Scale 1:250,000

Miles

OTHER STREAMS IN THE NORTH BRANCH
OF THE POTOMAC BASIN

NEW CREEK—9 Miles

MAPS: USGS—Antioch, Westernport, and Keyser
COUNTY—Mineral

Don't hold your breath on this one! This is about the absolute lower limit as far as size goes. When there is enough water on this tiny stream to float a boat, everything else has to be in flood stage. It is a straightforward Class 1-2 stream following major highways through largely pastoral settings. Other than the usual little stream difficulties, there are 2 low-water bridges and a 3-foot dam at the Keyser Water Works. Put in near the intersection of WV 93 and US 50 or anywhere else upstream or downstream as the highway is always close by. Take out on US 220 in Keyser near the Potomac State campus.

PATTERSON CREEK—23 Miles

MAPS: USGS—Burlington, Headsville, Cresaptown, and Patterson
Creek
COUNTIES—Grant and Mineral

This is an interesting stream passing through a very fertile, historic valley. It has been inhabited for centuries as evidenced by the wealth of Indian artifacts that may still be collected in the area. It is one of the richest areas of the state for game—with deer, squirrels, and wild turkey being especially plentiful. The small stream is also rich in bass and, surprisingly, muskies. Again, it is runnable only when everything else is up, but the riffles do not add up to any particular difficulty. As usual, the fences, dangling wires, etc., must be considered. A potentially interesting open-boat run could be made in high water between Burlington on US 50 and Fort Ashby at the intersection of WV 46 and WV 28, a distance of about 18 miles. It is another 5 miles to its mouth on the North Branch. There is a 4-foot dam just above WV 28 runnable on the left and a 2-foot dam about 2 miles downstream.

NORTH FORK OF PATTERSON CREEK—6.5 Miles

MAPS: USGS—Burlington
         COUNTY—Grant

The North Fork of Patterson Creek is very tiny, but at high water it affords a dashing run through Greenland Gap. Put-in is at the gravel pit above the Gap. Stream rushes continuously over ledges and boulders. Not surprisingly, trees could be a hazard here. There is a falls where the rock anticline of the Gap dips to the river. (Visible from the road through the Gap.) Take out 50 yards above, carry on the road, and put in at the bridge below. Below the Gap the river rushes over almost continuous gravel rapids through a beautiful pastoral valley. Besides many fences, there is a Soil Conservation Service impoundment just above the confluence with Patterson Creek. End your trip above the Dam (6.5 miles from the put-in) unless you plan to continue down Patterson Creek.

SOUTH BRANCH OF THE POTOMAC RIVER

A. The South Branch Above US 220 Bridge
Near Upper Tract—30+ Miles

MAPS: USGS—Upper Tract, Franklin, Sugar Grove, and Moatstown
             Monongahela National Forest
       COUNTY—Pendleton

The South Branch starts just inside Virginia with the confluence of Strait Creek and the East Branch Potomac River. Both of these tributaries are navigable by radical paddlers willing to portage dozens of fences. Reasonable paddlers can start at the forks. To Thorn Creek the stream is fairly busy, dropping gently over gravel bars, rock gardens, and a few ledges. At low levels a few diagonal gravel bars will be scrape-overs. Pools are short. You will encounter several barbed wire and wooden cattle fences and a few low-water bridges. The river flows through a pretty rural valley with many old houses and farm structures. Minimum level is about 4 feet on the Petersburg gauge. From Thorn Creek to US 220, minimum level would be about 3.5 feet at Petersburg. Here there are 4 low-water bridges and 2 cattle fences. There is a beautiful, short canyon just below Franklin. Watch for an old washed-out dam in the canyon. Just below the canyon is a 5-foot dam which should be carried. From this point on there are still many riffles, though the pools are longer. Franklin is an extremely attractive rural town with splendid overnight and eating facilities. It is the spelunking capital of West Virginia.

B. The Smoke Hole Run, US 220 to Petersburg—25 Miles

CLASS	GRADIENT	VOLUME	SCENERY	TIME	LEVEL
	5@35				
1–3$_4$	20@16	160	A	7	0–3′

MAPS: USGS—Petersburg and Onego 15′
       Monongahela National Forest
       COUNTIES—Pendleton and Grant

DESCRIPTION: This is a very long run, perhaps too much for one day, but it has been described collectively because it represents a sig-

South Branch of the Potomac River

nificantly identifiable unit even though many paddlers make a 2-day overnighter of it. The first 5 miles are unquestionably the best whitewater on the South Branch and among the most beautiful of the whole Potomac, a river system that has plenty of beauty. In spades! Some will argue that the extremely rugged mountains forming the lower Smoke Hole Canyon are even more beautiful. Don't argue, just enjoy.

The river begins to pick up speed and action as it leaves the broad valley below Franklin, passes under the US 220 bridge, and crosses a ford. It quickly turns a corner and enters a magnificent canyon which is a geologist's delight. The rapids through here are very closely spaced, fairly steep, and with enough complications to make your paddling interesting. Paddlers interested only in action will probably end their run after 5 miles at the Smoke Hole Campgrounds, but most will want to continue. Everyone should spend some time in this unique area as there are many attractive sights and trails in the area. Cave Mountain and Eagle Rock are 2 very noteworthy natural monuments.

Leaving the Smoke Hole Campgrounds, one enters the most scenic, most historic, and most famous run in West Virginia. This is the land of whiskey stills, Indian and Civil War battles, and, above all, mountaineer independence. For the most part, the river is running through an isolated canyon of unparalleled grandeur. Mountaineer farms and homesteads add to the charm of the run and remind the paddler of the fortitude and austerity of the early settlers. They also remind him of a tragic paradox. In order to protect the river for future generations from trash-laden riverbanks, fishing shanties, unplanned "developments" and the like, the Forest Service acquired this land to incorporate it into the Spruce Knob–Seneca Rocks National Recreation Area. In so doing, these independent farmers had to be displaced. It was unfortunate that their way of life could not be preserved since their clean and well-kept farms harmonize beautifully with the surroundings.

The rapids are not as heavy as those above and seldom exceed a Class 2 rating unless the water is very high. About 4 miles from the Smoke Hole Campgrounds the paddler will encounter the newly built Big Bend Campgrounds (both are operated by the Forest Service). This makes a convenient overnight spot since cars may be left here. It will be the last contact point until Royal Glen is reached miles below. From here on there are few signs of civilization, only the occasional remains of the old homesteads. Several excellent primitive campsites exist next to the deep pools. As the miles progress, the canyon and the gradient decrease, making longer pools between the rapids. Soon the

North Fork rushes in to join the parent stream and heads east toward Petersburg 4 miles away.

DIFFICULTIES: The major difficulty is encountered right off as one makes a right turn into the canyon. A massive rockslide is encountered where huge boulders block the river and the paddler's view, but this is easily seen and one has plenty of time to take out. Pull off to the right and scout. Either portage by following the yellow triangles or, if you are paddling a slalom boat, judiciously try it. At lower levels the only way is on the far left over a steep drop into a boiling washing machine, against a huge boulder, and then a very sharp turn to the right. Tough for left-handed paddlers. At high levels you are on your own. No immediate further difficulties will be encountered in the upper 5 miles except for heavy Class 3 rapids. At high levels you will have your hands full. Watch out for a low-water bridge at the picnic area. Portage necessary.

About 6 miles below the Big Bend Campground, a most unusual sight greets the paddler's eyes. An extremely massive landslide has occurred from high on the mountain on the left. This is Chimney Rock Slide and is visible for a considerable distance. The landslide has created a barrage on the river and a dangerous rapids. As you approach the rapids there is an island which you should run to the right of for portaging or scouting. The rapids is a short 10-foot drop over a boiling cascade. Under each pillow is a very sharp boulder, so the route through should be attempted only by very skilled paddlers. Running this in an open boat is not worth the risk.

As you approach the Royal Glen Dam, depending on the water level, you may want to land on the left and scout this, especially if you have an open boat. The dam is broken out on the left and can be run, but concrete reinforcing rods just below the surface make it dangerous, especially if they have entrapped logs and debris. The water going through the dam has tricky countercurrents which you may not be prepared for. The long rapids below here contains many high waves which could swamp an open boat loaded with camping equipment. Later, Smith Falls is encountered, which is a series of low ledges and hydraulics.

SHUTTLE: If you are planning on making the entire run either straight through or with an overnight out on the riverbank, the shuttle is simple. Just put in at the US 220 bridge below Upper Tract and take out at the next one in Petersburg, 15 miles away by car. Actually, a simpler put-in can be had by driving down to the ford just beyond the bridge. A short 5-mile run can be made by leaving a car at the Smoke Hole Campground and a 9-mile run by leaving it at the Big Bend Campground. Arranging a take-out at Royal Glen doesn't seem worth it in view of the horrendous shuttle which involves driving clear over the mountain on WV 74, turning on WV 4 and 28 to the right, and right again at the Department of Highway's maintenance yard. Great scenery up there but you may as well paddle the remaining 3.5 miles into Petersburg.

GAUGE: No really good one visible. Corbett and Matacia define an ideal level as water wetting the top of the low-water bridge at the Smoke Hole picnic area (4 miles from the put-in).* It can be run up to 8–10 inches less. If you can't see the bridge, be careful. The Petersburg gauge reading gives an approximation by deducting 3 feet.

C. Petersburg to Old Fields—17 Miles

CLASS	GRADIENT	VOLUME	SCENERY	TIME	LEVEL
1–2	8	672	B	4	0–2′

MAPS: USGS—Petersburg, Greenland Gap, and Moorefield 15′
COUNTIES—Grant and Hardy

DESCRIPTION: This is a flatter section of the upper Potomac traversing some of the finest agricultural land in West Virginia. The pools are long, and the gentle rapids (Class 1, occasionally 2) are few and far between. This is a good open-boat run through excellent fishing water. Bass and trout may be taken the year round.

The river branches many times below the US 220 bridge between Petersburg and Moorefield. In one of the major branches, known locally as "Buzzard's Fork," high rock formations on the left are interesting in that they are populated with what appear to be wild goats. To see them run up and down the sheer cliffs is worth the trip itself. Just below here on the left are 3 large pools of backwater than can be explored by canoe by short portages. Known as the "Sloughs," they are popular for bass fishing.

---

*H. Roger Corbett and Louis S. Matacia, *Blue Ridge Voyages*, vol. 2 (Rockville, Md.: Springriver Corp., 1972), 2.

South Branch of the Potomac River

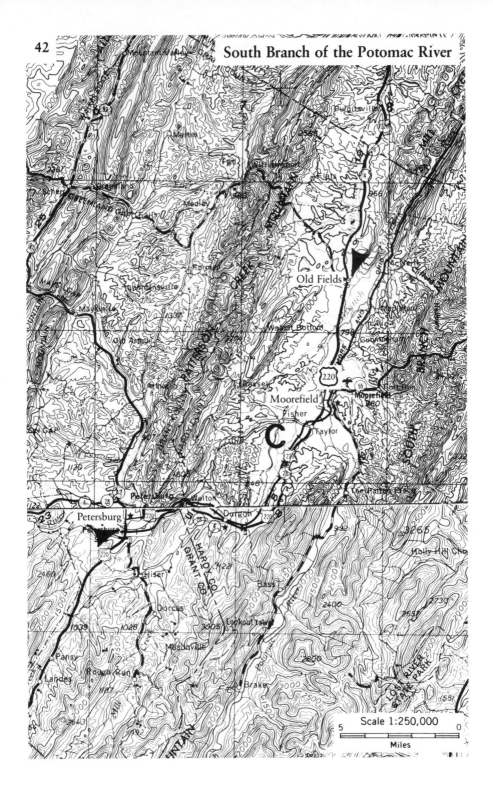

Old Fields

Moorefield
Fisher

C

Taylor

Petersburg

Dorgan

Scale 1:250,000

5   0

Miles

DIFFICULTIES: The only hazard to watch out for is a peculiarity of local laws and a few strange landowners. Apparently titles to the land in this area extend under the river, giving the landowner ownership of anything solid under the surface. This means if you flip, stop to dump, wade a riffle, or otherwise have to get out of your canoe, you are trespassing, and at least one person will have you arrested by a conservation officer if he catches you. It is pointless to test this strange situation, so please cooperate by staying in your boat.

SHUTTLE: Put in at the city parking lot in Petersburg and take out at the Old Fields bridge just north of Moorefield on US 220.

GAUGE: See section E, below.

D. The Trough—US 220 Bridge at Old Fields to Harmison's Landing—11 Miles

CLASS	GRADIENT	VOLUME	SCENERY	TIME	LEVEL
C, 1–2	5	1,226	A+	3	1.6–3.6'

MAPS: USGS—Moorefield and Keyser 15'
COUNTIES—Hardy and Hampshire

DESCRIPTION: This very beautiful and popular canoeing river, on which many organizations sponsor large float trips, is an ideal river for novices or even noncanoeists to run. The first 4 miles of the trip are through very scenic farmland and actually contain most of the rapids. The approach of the railroad bridge at the end of this stretch is tricky and marks the beginning of the Trough. As you make a wide, right-hand turn in the river, you are on the left side and must quickly get over to the right 50 yards above the bridge in order to avoid an exposed ledge. In high water there will be good-sized standing waves below the bridge for nearly 100 yards. You will then find yourself entering the serenity of a deep canyon with 1,500-foot mountain walls rising steeply from each side of the river. The vistas are ever changing and provide spectacular scenery, especially in the spring and fall when seasonal colors are at their peak. There is very little whitewater in the Trough itself, but the scenery more than makes up for this lack. This river also provides some of the best bass fishing in the state, and one can find many primitive campsites along the sandy banks. There are a few more riffles as one leaves the Trough, but the river has widened considerably. A must trip for every West Virginia outdoorsman. Other than a reasonable amount of caution at the railroad bridge, one need not worry about any difficulties.

SHUTTLE: See section E, below.

GAUGE: See section E, below.

E. Harmison's Landing to US 50 at Romney—13 Miles

CLASS	GRADIENT	VOLUME	SCENERY	TIME	LEVEL
1	5	1,226	A–B	4	2–4'

MAPS: USGS—Sector and Romney
COUNTY—Hampshire

DESCRIPTION: After leaving the Trough, the river widens and slows considerably. Within the next 10 miles, the river passes through verdant farmlands and is characterized by extremely long, placid pools punctuated by short riffles. It is an ideal float-fishing stream and is considered by some to be the best for trophy-sized bass. Nearing Romney, arising from the right bank and extending for more than a mile are shale cliffs which jut upward 200 feet. However, much of this prospect is spoiled by the camps and cottages perched atop the precipice. The trip from Harmison's Landing is ideal for novices, johnboats, and weekend campers. A popular 2-day, open-boat camping trip starts by putting in at the US 220 bridge, camping overnight at Harmison's, and then continuing on to Romney the next day. There are no difficulties in this lower part except an angry bull that will chase you if you get out at the wrong place.

SHUTTLE: The put-in for section D is easy to find—where US 220 crosses the South Branch just south of Old Fields—but finding the take-out at the end of the Trough (Harmison's Landing) isn't easy. Take the secondary road leading straight east from the put-in bridge, cross the railroad tracks, and turn left on the road at the farmhouse (it will be called "6" in Hardy County and "8" in Hampshire County). Continue on this road until the river comes back into view. Stop at either farmhouse on the right and request permission of Mr. Harmison to use the landing. There is a minimal canoe charge, and all canoeists are requested to honor this. The charge also covers camping for the night. Continuing on this same road will bring the shuttler to US 50.

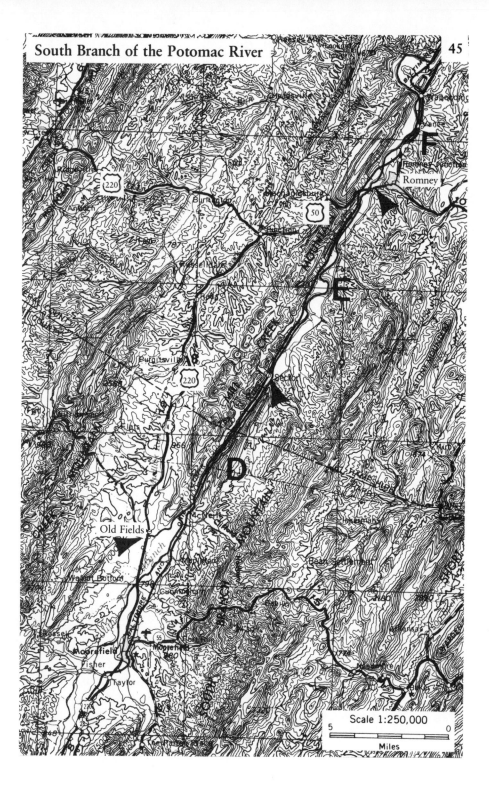

Scale 1:250,000

5   0

Miles

One can take out at the old bridge pier on the right bank 100 yards upstream from the present span.

GAUGE: Call (301) 899-3210 and listen for the Springfield gauge reading following the recorded weather report.

F. The South Branch Below Romney—34 Miles

MAPS: USGS—Augusta, Springfield, Levels, and Oldtown
       COUNTY—Hampshire

There is little of interest to the whitewater paddler in the long, slow 34-mile stretch of the South Branch to its junction with the North Branch at Green Spring. There is very little action, the banks are pretty muddy, and the scenery consists of fairly developed farmland or fishing shanties. It is a good float-fishing stream and well recommended for bass, but it may get dangerous at high-water stages.

MOOREFIELD RIVER

A. Fort Seybert to Milam Bridge—10 Miles

CLASS	GRADIENT	VOLUME	SCENERY	TIME	LEVEL
2–4	25(4 @ 40)	204	A–B	3	1–3'

MAPS: USGS—Fort Seybert and Petersburg
        COUNTIES—Pendleton and Hardy

DESCRIPTION: The whole trip is characterized by fantastic beauty. All of the headwaters of the Potomac are characterized by massive rock formations that are awe-inspiring, and the Moorefield (also called the South Fork of the South Branch of the Potomac) ranks among the best. The water is magnificently clear and the banks absolutely unlittered. The wildlife to be seen is abundant—ducks, turkeys, beaver, kingfishers, woodchucks, and deer may be seen on a single trip. Yet, as of this writing, this magnificent gorge is considered to be a choice spot for one of an eastern electric company's pumped storage projects. The cost of kilowatt hours could never be high enough to pay for this unique setting.

DIFFICULTIES: After a couple of miles from the put-in and just past a little church on the right, the river divides into 3 channels. One encounters a pretty mean rapids, choked by boulders, when they come together again. If you don't like this, you had better quit because it is only a prelude to what lies ahead in the canyon. Next follows an extremely beautiful cruise through a farm valley (Class 2). The farms, though isolated, are very well kept and progressive. At the end of this valley, a massive rock formation on the right stands as a sentinel guarding the entrance of the Moorefield Gorge. For the next 4 miles the rapids are steep, steeper than the gradient indicates because there are many flat pools between each set, and many are mean.

Most of the rapids are choked by huge boulders, obscuring the paddler's vision. He must either paddle them by the seat of his pants or else do some judicious scouting. The latter is recommended, particularly in high water. Take your time through here, for safety's sake as well as for the enjoyment of the incredible beauty.

SHUTTLE: The take-out is 2 miles south of Milam (upstream) on "7/3" almost at the county line. The put-in is just a few more miles

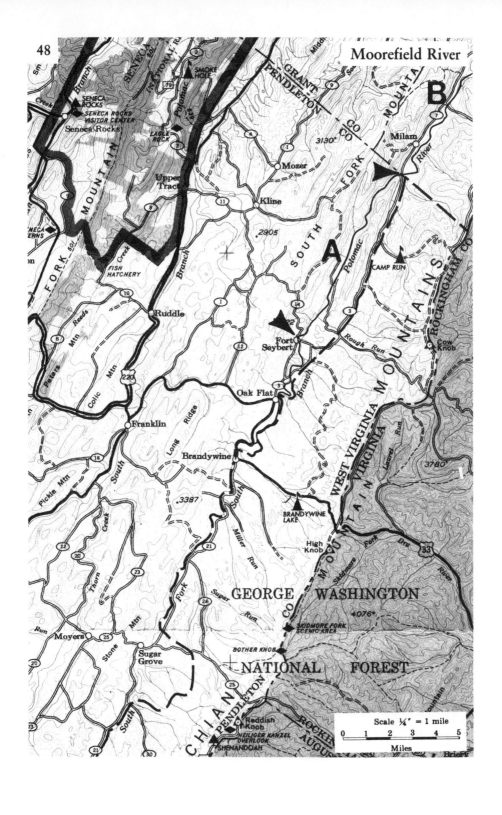

Scale ¼" = 1 mile

0   1   2   3   4   5

Miles

south at the bridge at Fort Seybert on Pendleton "7" (same road). One of the easiest shuttles.

GAUGE: There is a yellow painted gauge on the Milam bridge. There is also a gauge on the US 20 bridge in Moorefield that roughly correlates. An approximation is 4.5–6' on the Springfield gauge; call (301) 899-3210 for a reading.

B. The Moorefield Below the Milam Bridge — 25 miles

MAPS: USGS — Milam, Petersburg East, Lost River State Park, and Moorefield
         COUNTY — Hardy

DESCRIPTION: This is a delightful open-boat trip through some of the most charming farmland in West Virginia. The small river winds placidly through the pastoral scenery with enough short, straightforward rapids to make things interesting. The rapids are more numerous at the upper end but become sparser toward Moorefield.

DIFFICULTIES: There are numerous low-water bridges that need to be carried and which could be dangerous in high water. Immediately downstream from one of these concrete bridges, different from the rest in that it is characterized by arches instead of holes, is a more difficult rapids than usual caused by large boulders in midstream. Except for this, the whole stream has a Class 1–2 rating and is very narrow throughout.

SHUTTLE: Milam can be reached by taking the South Branch River Road "7" south of Moorefield. The bridge is another couple of miles south of Milam. Take out either at the bridge in Moorefield or continue 3 more miles to the Old Fields bridge on the South Branch (US 220). Since the river is never very far from the highway, many shorter trips on this small stream are possible.

GAUGE: Readjusted yellow numbers on the Milam bridge are still too low. Don't run unless you have at least a foot. (Based on a scouting report as well as experience with the upper river.)

NORTH FORK OF SOUTH BRANCH OF THE POTOMAC

A. Circleville to Mouth of Seneca Creek—16 Miles

CLASS	GRADIENT	VOLUME	SCENERY	TIME	LEVEL
1–2₃	34	S	B	4	3–6'

MAPS: USGS—Circleville, Onego, and Upper Tract
Monongahela National Forest
COUNTY—Pendleton

DESCRIPTION: This is a zestful little stream that flows rather straightforwardly through an extremely scenic valley and hugs the base of North Fork Mountain. The rapids at lower water levels are mostly Class 2 but could get very interesting if the water were high. Mostly continuous action, although there are a few long, flat pools.

DIFFICULTIES: Below Riverton a fairly high ledge or small falls is encountered which has at least 2 good, obvious passages. Just above this a fairly large uprooted sycamore has fallen across the river, thus blocking a very choice passage. In 1975 a kayaker was pinned under this tree and drowned. *Stay away from fallen trees as the current does not!* You may be strained out like wet tea leaves. About a mile above the take-out one begins to find things picking up to Class 3. This is due to the many series of small ledges that cut across the river at 30- to 45-degree angles, thus providing some interesting sport. Watch for a low-water bridge near Riverton.

SHUTTLE: The whole run is never very far from the highway, so numerous choices can be made for trips of various lengths. Put in at the bridge at the edge of Circleville. You can take out at bridges at Judy Gap, Riverton, or on the Harper's Gap road (CR 9) just beside Hedrick's Motel. Take out at the parking lot where the swinging bridge crosses over to Seneca Rocks.

GAUGE: See section D, below.

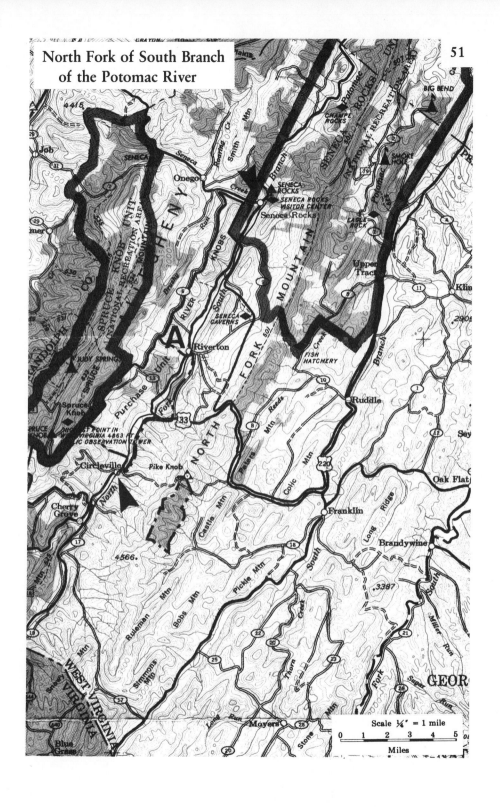

North Fork of South Branch
of the Potomac River

B. Mouth of Seneca to Dolly Camp Grounds—10 Miles

CLASS	GRADIENT	VOLUME	SCENERY	TIME	LEVEL
1–2	22	S–M	B	2–3	2.4–5′

MAPS: USGS—Upper Tract and Hopeville
Monongahela National Forest
COUNTY—Pendleton

DESCRIPTION: This was the site of the Cruiser Class race at the annual Whitewater Weekend. This river is a most attractive one and a very solid, continuous Class 2 run at medium water heights. Almost every conceivable type of Class 1–2 rapids appears on this river; numerous fast rapids, large waves, and the main current frequently take the paddler under overhanging branches and through long rock gardens, zesty chutes, sharp turns, and even a ledge. This is a tremendous run seemingly designed to test the beginning-to-intermediate paddler's mettle and repertoire of strokes. This unquestionably is some of West Virginia's finest canoeing and has probably been run by more canoeists than any other single river in the state.

Some of the state's most breathtaking scenery can be seen from this section of the Potomac. Seneca and Champe Rocks are in the immediate vicinity, while the imposing majesties of Allegheny Front and North Fork Mountain loom in the distance on either side of the river, providing a splendid backdrop for canoeing. Excellent trout and bass fishing can be had on this clear, unpolluted river, but its proximity to the road and numerous vacation cabins place the fragile beauty of the river in a precarious position.

Because of the popularity of this section of the Potomac, some landowners have become irate at abuses to their property and fences by inconsiderate trespassers. Pick public access points or be very judicious and ask permission for other areas. This caution also applies to the other sections described herein. It is reportedly these abuses and the overrunning of the area, often by nonpaddlers, during the very popular Whitewater Weekend that has forced the cancellation and relocation of the races.

DIFFICULTIES: Actually there are no really bad places, but a canoeist does tend to remember places where he has gotten into trouble in the past. One of these occurs just downstream from Yokum's Motel. The stream splits, and the only passable channel is to the right. Overhanging branches or a fallen tree often add spice to the tight passage. About halfway the river appears to run through the woods. Apparently the course of the river has been changed due to natural causes in recent years, and it hasn't yet made up its mind which way to go. Thus choosing the correct passage quickly without previous knowledge is not easy, and past experience may not be a completely reliable guide. Watch for this tricky spot shortly after passing an aluminum painted bus along the left shore.

About three-quarters of the way into the trip the river is flowing through trees on the left as it turns left around a point and through a stopper. Just past the stopper there appears to be a flat pool, but actually a very deceptive ledge splits the pool. This has flipped many an unwary paddler. The only passage in low or medium water is way over against the left bank under an overhanging tree.

SHUTTLE: Put in under the bridge over Seneca Creek on WV 28. This stream joins the North Fork in a few hundred yards. Take out above Dolly Camp Grounds near the Grant-Pendleton County line. Dolly Camp Grounds is private land; put in and take out by permission only—get in touch with the owner, Mr. Ernest Dolly.

GAUGE: See section D, below.

C. Dolly Camp Grounds to Smoke Hole Caverns—5 miles

CLASS	GRADIENT	VOLUME	SCENERY	TIME	LEVEL
2–3	33	M	A	1	2.3–5'

MAPS: USGS—Hopeville
       Monongahela National Forest
       COUNTY—Grant

DESCRIPTION: The Hopeville Canyon section of the North Fork is a real thriller and can get pretty interesting in high water. This 5-mile section has been the site of the Championship Downriver Class Race, held annually during the first weekend in April. It is a good river for intermediates to test their capability of moving on to advanced paddling. The rapids are all steep and require precise maneuvering around the boulders. It is definitely more difficult than anything appearing in the upper portions of the river, and it has considerably more volume than above Mouth of Seneca.

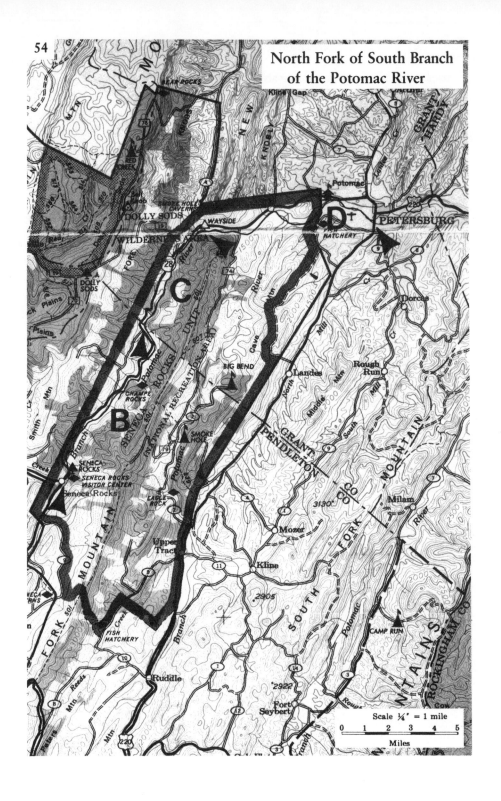

North Fork of South Branch
of the Potomac River

Scale ¼" = 1 mile

0   1   2   3   4   5

Miles

DIFFICULTIES: There are at least 16 rapids in the canyon and a few more near the road before getting to the take-out. It is difficult to describe any of the upper Potomac headwaters because they are still in the making, i.e., the rivers traverse such sheer canyons, the walls of which are subject to erosion and, inevitably, landslides. The North Fork has been changed often because of this. In late winter 1971, a massive landslide from the left cliff created a new rapids. The slide is easily recognized as the new rapids drops out of sight (literally and figuratively). Scout on the right. By 1972 the newly deposited rocks had been shifted again. Look out for Piton Rock high in the rapids. Start on the right and get left. The bottom obstructing boulders of 1971 have now been rolled to benign positions.

SHUTTLE: Easily made on WV 28. Put in above Dolly Camp Grounds and take out by the remnants of a primitive bridge at Smoke Hole Caverns Campground. (See comments on shuttle in previous section.)

GAUGE: See section D, below.

D. Smoke Hole Caverns to Petersburg—9 Miles

CLASS	GRADIENT	VOLUME	SCENERY	TIME	LEVEL
1–3	20	M	B	2+	4.5'

MAPS: USGS—Hopeville and Petersburg West
        Monongahela National Forest
        COUNTY—Grant

DESCRIPTION: This run into Petersburg is not paddled very often, but it contains some nice water. Many of the rapids are visible from the road, but soon the river takes off to join its mama, the South Branch fresh out of Smoke Hole country. The river passes through fairly open, well-kept farmland, and although it is leaving the mountains behind, there are still some spectacular scenes to come, particularly at the place known as Royal Glen, the site of an old broken-out dam.

Unfortunately, the Corps of Engineers considers the narrowness of this steep pass a naturally groovy spot for one of their concrete tombstones. Remember this if you have enjoyed your run either on the North Fork or on the lower Smoke Hole Run of the South Branch.

One of the Corps' plans would have flooded the North Fork halfway through the Hopeville Canyon and the entire South Branch–lower Smoke Hole run almost back to the campgrounds.

DIFFICULTIES: Where the North Fork joins the South Branch, it divides into several channels, some of which may be obstructed by logs or fallen trees. The old broken-out Royal Glen Dam may be run on the left with caution. Concrete reinforcing rods lurk just below the surface and may have trapped debris. The countercurrent below the chute is tricky. The long rapids immediately below here are not tricky but may have some pretty good-sized waves. Further down toward Petersburg the paddler will encounter an entertaining staircase of riverwide ledges which deserve the usual caution regarding possible hydraulics.

SHUTTLE: Put in across from the Smoke Hole Caverns (worth a trip in themselves) on WV 28 and take out on the left bank before the bridge in Petersburg. This is next to the big parking lot and city park adjacent to the Petersburg fire hall.

GAUGE: For all sections, call (301) 899-3210 and listen for the Petersburg reading following the recorded weather forecast. This is the gauge referred to in all sections above. There is a visual canoeing gauge painted on the rock on the far side of the river at Harman's Pool, located at the end of the canyon at the tourist cabins. You will need at least 1.5 feet for section A on this canoeist's gauge. Three feet is a good maximum for all sections on this crude gauge. The differential between the government gauge at Petersburg and the canoeist's gauge is 2.3 feet. Some variation can be expected since the Petersburg gauge also includes the South Branch discharge.

SENECA CREEK

Forest Service Campgrounds to WV 28 Bridge—6 Miles

CLASS	GRADIENT	VOLUME	SCENERY	TIME	LEVEL
3	70–90	S	B	3	2–3'

MAPS: USGS—Onego 15'
       Monongahela National Forest
       COUNTY—Pendleton

DESCRIPTION: Born high on West Virginia's tallest mountain, this lively little ripsnorter is pure delight if you can catch it up. Often after early spring thaws one can find suitable levels. It is essentially a 6-mile-long rapids with but 1 or 2 very short pools breaking up the waves. The course is extremely narrow, especially in the upper parts, and very fast. However, there is very little maneuvering required since there are few obstructions. You just skirt up and go. The course traverses pastoral farmlands around the northern edge of Spruce Mountain and heads east toward the imposing majesty of Seneca Rocks.

DIFFICULTIES: Very few at the levels indicated. Just above and just below the Onego bridge are some sloping ledges into some hydraulics that demand a reasonable amount of attention. About 300 yards downstream from a small white church there is a dangling cable that threatens to decapitate the busy paddler. Pass on either side. About a half mile downstream one encounters 2 pools that run out sharply to the left and S curve to the right. Each of these has a big hydraulic right in the main channel. Within view of Seneca Rocks one notices the banks littered with discarded cars and encounters Junkyard Falls, an otherwise beautiful 8-foot staircase descent into fairly turbulent water. Overhanging branches or downed trees offer the only other hazards at medium levels.

SHUTTLE: Put in at the USFS Seneca Campgrounds, which incidentally is an ideal spot for a base camp when paddling in this area. Take out at the left side of the WV 28 bridge, the put-in for the Petersburg Cruiser Race.

GAUGE: The level referred to above was from a gauge located under the left side of the bridge at the Seneca Campgrounds. It was washed out in 1974 and has yet to be replaced. The best predictor at present is a 4- to 8-foot level at Petersburg.

OTHER STREAMS IN THE SOUTH BRANCH
OF THE POTOMAC BASIN

LUNICE CREEK — 10 Miles

MAPS: USGS — Maysville and Rig
　　　　COUNTY — Grant

This very shallow, small trout stream can occasionally be run from near the vicinity of Maysville all the way into the South Branch at Petersburg near the tannery. It can be run when the water is very high elsewhere and affords fairly continuous Class 1–2 action.

THORN CREEK — 7.5 Miles

MAPS: USGS — Sugar Grove
　　　　Monongahela National Forest
　　　　COUNTY — Pendleton

This little headwater tributary to the South Branch has 7.5 miles of Class 2–3 water from near Moyers to the mouth. At a left turn 2.5 miles into the trip there are 2 interesting rapids, the second of which is blocked by a log. At the mouth is a terrible looking 5-foot ledge. Paddle this when the Petersburg gauge nears 5 feet. There are lots of limestone and caves along the run.

THE MAIN STEM OF THE POTOMAC—115 Miles

MAPS: USGS—Old Town, Paw Paw, Great Cacapon, Bellgrove, Hancock, Cherry Run, Big Pool, Hedgesville, Williamsport, Shepardstown, Keedyville, Charles Town, and Harpers Ferry
COUNTIES—Hampshire, Morgan, Berkeley, and Jefferson

DESCRIPTION: From 2 miles below Green Spring, West Virginia (Oldtown, Maryland), where the North and South branches of the Potomac meet to form the great Potomac River, the beautiful, historic West Virginia–Maryland border river flows majestically for almost 115 miles toward Harpers Ferry. The river in most places is suitable for well-coached beginners in open boats. It is mostly flat water, but there are occasional Class 1–2 riverwide rapids. It should be remembered that this is a huge river and the force behind the little waves is considerable. It is an extremely dangerous river in high water.

The historic Chesapeake and Ohio Canal follows the Maryland shore, and at several points, historic or restored remains are worth visiting. In addition, a well-maintained hiking and cycling trail follows the old tow path on the left bank. Civil War battlefields and Revolutionary War sites add further historic interest to canoe runs in this area. Several developed campsites exist along the river which one can use as bases for canoeing operations. Obtaining a copy of *Hiker's Guide to the C and O Canal* is highly recommended. It can be purchased from the Mason-Dixon Council of the Boy Scouts, 1200 Crestwood Drive, Hagerstown, MD 21740. This book is crammed with information about historic sites, camping areas, roads, and other points of interest in the area which the canoeist would find invaluable in planning his trip.

A highly recommended camping location is Fort Frederick State Park in Maryland, south of Hagerstown. It is the site of a historic Revolutionary War fort and a particularly impressive portion of the canal. Historic Antietam Battlefield is nearby. Finally, of course, the river is beautiful here, containing interesting, closely spaced rapids, and teeming in wildlife, especially waterfowl.

The National Park Service is rebuilding and developing much of the canal into a national monument. One of the places scheduled for development in West Virginia is near Paw Paw on WV 29. It is a shame

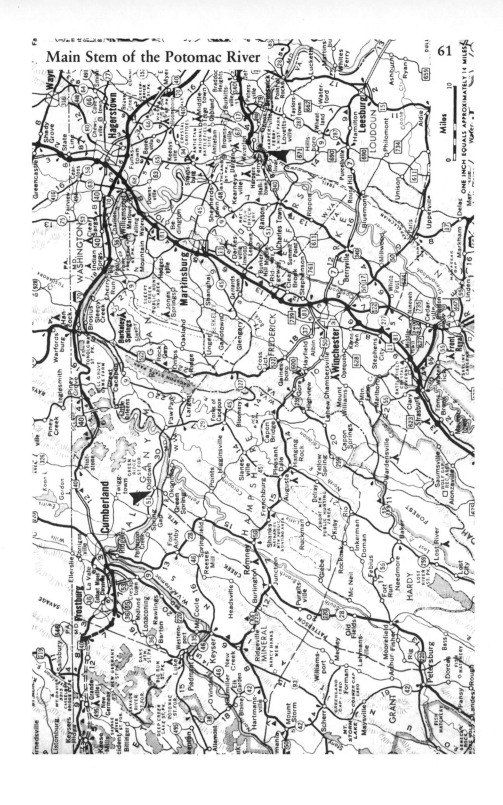

the state has never developed a state park along this magnificently beautiful and historic river.

DIFFICULTIES: Several of the old C and O dams still remain. Dam No. 6 just above the mouth of the Cacapon is broken out. About 10 miles below Fort Frederick, No. 5 creates a 5-mile-long lake and must be portaged on the West Virginia side. There is a power plant dam right below Williamsport, Maryland. Dam No. 4 is a high one creating a 13-mile-long lake (Big Slackwater) and is located near Falling Waters, West Virginia. The last dam in West Virginia is No. 3, which backs up water for 5 miles above Harpers Ferry.

The 2 miles of the Potomac below Dam No. 3 down to Harpers Ferry, the mouth of the Shenandoah, and 1 mile farther to Sandy Hook, Maryland, below the US 340 bridge, are definitely not for beginners. This beautiful stretch, called the Needles, is wide and powerful and almost continuous Class 1–2. If the river is high, it could be dangerous. A flipped or swamped boat could be very difficult to get out of or, with high water and cold temperature, *impossible* for the novice. A half mile below Harpers Ferry, White Horse Rapids appears on the left side of the river. Here one will find the biggest waves on this section, and although they are regular, they are powerful. There are many rocky islands in this same area inviting other routes. The river on the right consists of small ledges between these islands.

SHUTTLE: Because of the many different trips that could be imagined or planned for this very long section of river, the best advice seems to be to consult your West Virginia and Maryland road maps for major access points or the above-mentioned county maps for more detail.

GAUGE: The Hancock gauge gives a good estimation; call (301) 899-3210. Beginners should consider 2–4 feet as ideal. The river becomes high and dangerous between 5–7 feet and above.

LOST RIVER

WV 55 Bridge Above Wardensville to WV 259 Bridge Below Wardensville—6 Miles

CLASS	GRADIENT	VOLUME	SCENERY	TIME	LEVEL
2–4	40	S	B	2	1.5′+

MAPS: USGS—Wardensville 15′
COUNTY—Hardy

DESCRIPTION: This section of the Lost River, called the Dry Gorge section, is the most unique and best-named river in the state in that it doesn't always exist! In low water the river actually disappears into the ground just beyond the bridge above Wardensville, thus leaving it indeed dry for most of the year. The river apparently traverses some unknown Stygian course only to emerge several miles away, seemingly *de novo*, to form the Cacapon River.

DIFFICULTIES: A run on this section can therefore only be made in high water when the underground river can't handle all of the flow and the river spills over into the flood channel cut around the mountain. Fantastic! For the first couple of miles there are frequent Class 2–3 rapids. Two islands mark a landslide-choked channel necessitating a carry. Below the islands there is a series of steep ledges with their accompanying hydraulics. This is very steep and can be really mean in high water. Run these just to the right of center as there is a low-water bridge right below them which must be portaged on the right. There are many chutes and drops through narrow passages that require maneuvering back and forth across the river to find the next passage, and another low-water bridge must be carried near the end of the flood channel (on the right).

Soon the point is reached at which the underwater river miraculously reappears from a series of small springs and the volume of the river fascinatingly doubles. Where the flood channel and the underground river merge, there is another series of steep ledges which produces heavier rapids than the first series. There are also several more good rapids before reaching the take-out bridge. From here on, the river, now called the Cacapon, is much tamer. Catching the Dry Gorge wet is difficult but well worth the wait.

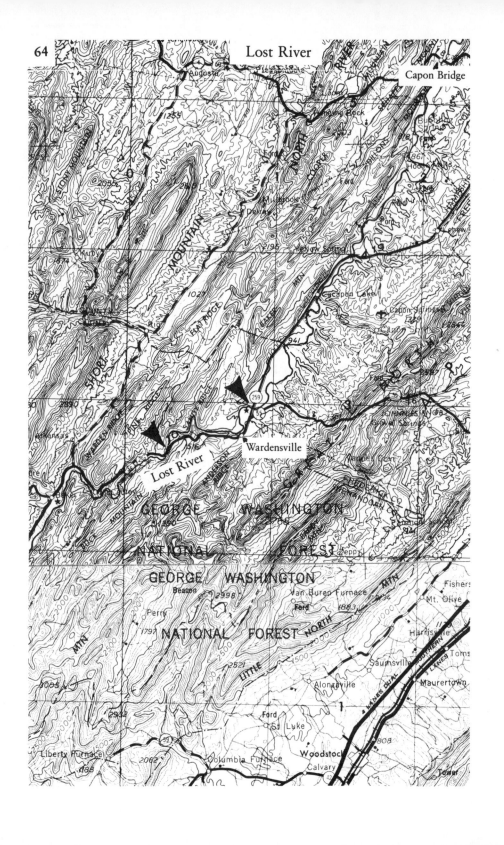

Capon Bridge

Wardensville

Lost River

SHUTTLE: Very simple—use the WV 55 bridge upstream of Wardensville and take out at the WV 259 bridge downstream of Wardensville or at the low-water bridge off WV 55 above Wardensville to eliminate some flat water.

GAUGE: Check the gauge under the US 50 bridge at the town of Capon Bridge. This reading may be obtained from the Coryell Market, 856-2750. There is a painted gauge at the upper bridge above Wardensville. A reading of 2.5 feet on this gauge is enough. The Cootes Store gauge on the North Fork of Shenandoah is an indication of area discharge. Look for a 3- to 6-foot range.

CACAPON RIVER

A. The Cacapon Above Capon Bridge (US 50) — 30 Miles

MAPS: USGS — Wardensville, Yellow Spring, Capon Springs, and
Capon Bridge
COUNTIES — Hardy and Hampshire

The long section of the Cacapon River from Wardensville to US 50 offers little in the way of whitewater except for occasional riffles in medium water. It is, however, a good bass fishing stream and is popular, if not ideal, for float fishing. A good secondary road follows the river from Capon Bridge to Yellow Spring, and from there to Wardensville, WV 259 is handy. Hence, many shorter trips are possible. The pools in many instances are long and deep and at least one is the remains of an old millpond impoundment. Unfortunately this section of the river has been turned into essentially a rural slum in many places due to the unlimited and closely spaced vacation cabins and trailers that line the banks, some in unbelievably poor taste. Sewage from these places as well as towns upstream has caused great increases in algal growth in recent years. A myth persists that the Cacapon is one of the few rivers in the state where you can still drink right from the river. The reverse would be closer to the truth.

A good way to judge the water level in this section is to check the riffles across the road from the Cacapon Restaurant on US 55 Wardensville. If this is runnable, so is everything else.

B. Capon Bridge to WV 127 Bridge — 12 Miles

CLASS	GRADIENT	VOLUME	SCENERY	TIME	LEVEL
1–3	14	549	A	4	1–3′

MAPS: USGS — Capon Bridge
COUNTY — Hampshire

DESCRIPTION: This is a very popular eastern canoeing stream that contains exquisite scenery and challenging whitewater for the intermediate paddler. It is a good float-fishing stream for open boats, but would require skills well beyond that of the novice to negotiate safely. It has drowned foolish, inexperienced paddlers. It is often up in the winter, and the snow-covered banks combined with the unusual rock formations make this a highly recommended run for the experienced paddler.

The trip begins with flat water and a few riffles flowing through open farmland. After about 3 miles, the river heads to the left past high rocky cliffs and things get a little more interesting. There are 3 small- to medium-sized ledges that require skill and possibly scouting for correct passage. Toward the end of the run, a spectacular rock formation, Caudy's Castle, may be seen high on the left. It is well worth an exploratory side trip. From here on to the bridge you'll find a good deal of flat water.

DIFFICULTIES: The first low ledge, at the end of a right-hand turn with a cliff on the left, is best run on the far right in lower water. Right below this is a nice sandy beach suitable for lunch stops. The second ledge is at the end of a spectacular rock formation called "Chapel Rock" and is always runnable on the far left. The third ledge is sort of big, and intermediate paddlers may want to scout. In low water the passage is on the right, but at the risk of banging your stern pretty hard. At 9 inches or more the best passage is just left of center, but it requires more skill in maneuvering.

SHUTTLE: Put in under the US 50 bridge on the left (which is rather steep) or drive down the left side of the river 3 miles to Cold Stream for a riverside put-in that cuts off mostly flat water. Take out on the right under the WV 127 bridge. It's a difficult climb. To reach this from Cold Stream, simply continue to Slanesville on "15" and "45/20," turn right on WV 29 and on to WV 127. Be sure to leave your car at the second bridge. (The first is over the North River.)

GAUGE: Both bridges have canoeing gauges, but one cannot improve on Roger Corbett and Louis Matacia's advice which warns against scraping on the first riffle below the US 50 bridge (can be estimated by inspection). The Cacapon is simply boring if the water is too low. At such levels taking a hike is more rewarding. Gauge readings may be obtained from the Coryell Market at Capon Bridge, 856-2750. The Cootes Store gauge on Shenandoah's north fork should be in the 3- to 5-foot range.

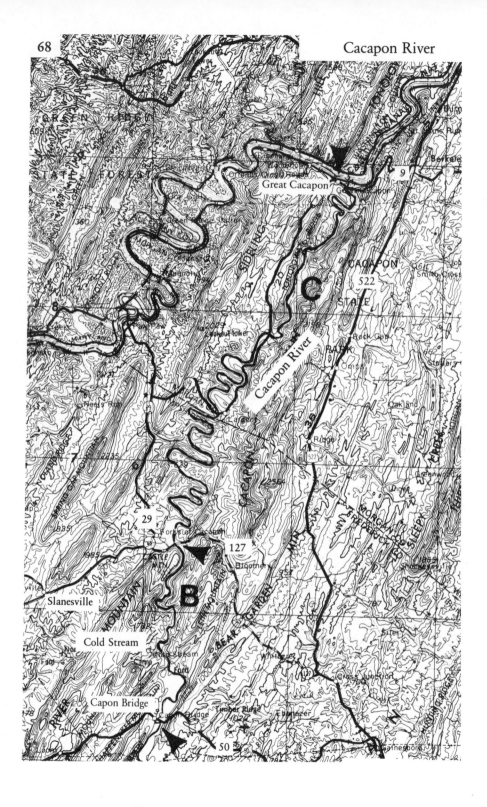

C. The Cacapon Below WV 127 to Potomac River—40 Miles

MAPS: USGS—Largent and Great Cacapon
          COUNTIES—Hampshire and Morgan

The river below the WV 127 bridge has very little gradient all of the way to the mouth of the Potomac at Great Cacapon. It transcribes huge loops through the mountains and ridges with very few rapids and many long, flat pools. As such it is an ideal float-fishing stream and even amateur anglers will tell you that it contains some of the best bass fishing water in the state. (Hint: use eels, live or artificial, for bait. Catfish minnows are also good.) Much of the scenery down to Largent is pretty good, but there are a lot of vacation cabins and summer homes along the way. These are apparently owned by a much wealthier class of people than those above US 50, judging by the expensive appearance of many of them. New trailer parks and fishing camps are going in everyday. (Is this what is to become of all West Virginia rivers?) Largent may be reached from near the WV 127 bridge by taking WV 29 north to WV 9 and then turning right. Continue straight on WV 9 to Great Cacapon. The only difficulty to warn you about is a high dam about 4 miles above Great Cacapon. Carry on the left. Also, landowners are very particular about having paddlers camp on their lands because of the many abuses in the past, so always check first. The river is incredibly rich in wildlife; it is not unusual to see beaver, wild turkeys, and deer in a short period of time. If you are making a float trip, we advise getting on the river at daybreak to take advantage of this. Eat your breakfast at mid-morning. The state of West Virginia has constructed access areas at WV 9, Great Cacapon, at WV 127, and at Cold Stream.

SHENANDOAH RIVER

A. VA 7 to Bloomery Road near WV 9—13 Miles

MAPS: USGS—Round Hill
         COUNTIES—Clarke, Va. and Jefferson

This is a good beginner's run because it is easy, smooth water run-nable even in the driest summer, and it is within range of several canoe liveries. There are occasional riffles formed by low limestone ledges or old fishtrap weirs. These wash out at moderate water levels (3 feet at Millville USGS gauge). The scenery is pleasant though not outstand-ing. Banks are often high and treelined, and where they give way to bluffs, look for caves. There are also some views of the Blue Ridge to the east. Put in at the Virginia Game Commission access area at VA 7 bridge, and take out along Bloomery Road below WV 9. The shuttle routes are also quite scenic.

Minimum level might be 1.0 foot at Front Royal or 1.5 feet at Millville, although even lower is probably tolerable due to its flatness.

B. Bloomery Road to Millville—3.5 Miles

MAPS: USGS—Round Hill and Charles Town
         COUNTY—Jefferson

This section is seldom run. Put in below WV 9 where Bloomery Road leaves the river. This is at the head of a short, interesting, ledgy (staircase) rapids, Class 2. Enjoy it while you can because it is followed by a wide, mile-long pool formed by a 20-foot power dam. This is a masonry structure extended a few feet higher by a wooden crest, and at low levels (Millville USGS gauge 2 feet or less), the water flows under the crest rather than over it. At such levels paddle to the left edge of the dam and you'll find a wooden ramp down which you can portage. Higher levels mean a potentially arduous portage on the left on power company property. Be sure you can see the wooden crest before approaching the brink of the dam. Below the dam are some genuinely interesting staircase ledges which unfortunately soon give way to the pool at Millville. Minimum level, 1.7 on the Millville gauge.

C. Millville to Sandy Hook, Maryland—7 Miles

CLASS	GRADIENT	VOLUME	SCENERY	TIME	LEVEL
	$\frac{1}{4}@30$				
$1-2_3$	$\frac{1}{2}@20$	2,588	A–B	2	$2-4'+$

MAPS: USGS—Charles Town and Harpers Ferry
       COUNTIES—Jefferson and Loudoun, Va.

DESCRIPTION: This is a tremendously beautiful river no matter how you look at it. The river passes between majestic cliffs; winds through interesting islands; provides homes and resting places for an incredible variety of waterfowl; passes along the historic, nineteenth-century charm of Harpers Ferry and the site of John Brown's fateful escapade; and finally joins the mighty Potomac through a magnificent gap in the Blue Ridge, the last water to bathe West Virginia mountains.

The fabled Shenandoah Staircase may be seen just under and upstream from the US 340 bridge in Harpers Ferry. Like many rivers in the Eastern Panhandle, the rapids here are formed by the sharp upthrusting ends of sedimentary rock. This creates a long, interesting series of ledges that spans the entire river diagonally from right to left and provides the boater with a variety of entertainment under fairly safe conditions. The paddler can find a passage, eddy turn, ferry in either direction, find the next passage, and so on. The force of the river at normal levels (0–2 feet) and the shallow waters remind one of the rapids below the Hinton bridge on the New River. Of course, if the river is high it can be powerful and dangerous.

This is an excellent place for the whole family, regardless of their interests. Some people just like to climb one of the many cliffs in the area, sit on a rock, and watch the river and the day go by. Even though the water pollution is irritatingly noticeable at low water and the river is located so far from the bulk of the state's paddlers (3½ hours from Morgantown, 8 from Charleston!), it is a must for every West Virginian.

DIFFICULTIES: Not too many, aside from getting there. The river begins as flat water, and the first rapids begins against a high cliff as the river turns to the right. The good water is on the left. The river then pools up behind a riverwide barrage, Bull Falls, which is a 3- to 4-foot ledge containing many passages. The ones on the left contain

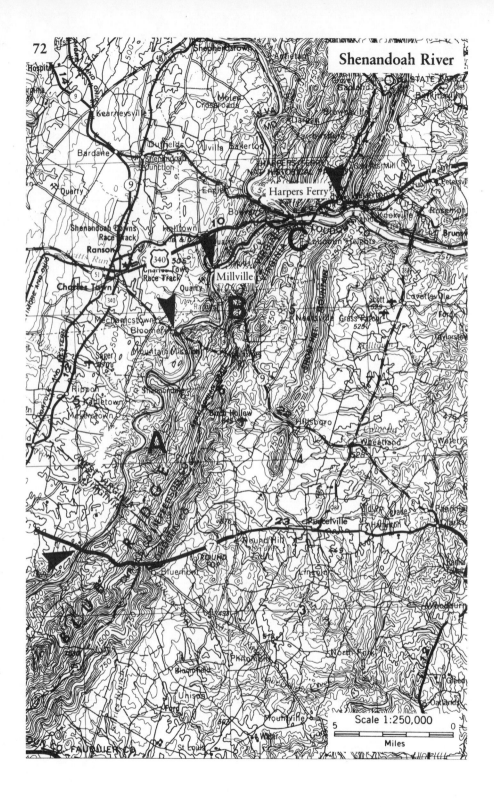

Shenandoah River

Scale 1:250,000

Miles

the heaviest water, and the ones on the right may not have enough unless the river is high. The novice may do well to scout this first. There will be at least 1 hydraulic and a series of haystacks below each passage. Another nice 100-yard descent follows immediately and will be rather turbulent at levels over 1.0 foot.

The Staircase, already described, is next, with the heaviest water just under and below the bridge. After joining the Potomac, the paddler should be mindful that the volume has now more than doubled and even the smallest waves are powerful. About a half mile below this junction, White Horse Rapids is encountered on the left which is a set of pretty good standing waves. Flips here are common and rescues difficult in high water.

SHUTTLE: Put-in is reached by driving west of Harpers Ferry on US 340 and turning left at the first interchange to Millville (marked by a sign to the right, "Harpers Ferry Caverns"). Put in at the pump house at river level. Take out at the Potomac Wayside Area at the Virginia end of the US 340 bridge (over the Potomac). If you want to run the Needles of the Potomac (see page 62), continue exactly 2 miles up the road from Sandy Hook to a convenient put-in.

GAUGE: Use the Millville gauge reading (don't confuse with the staff gauge on the pump house at the put-in). Usually figure on at least 2 feet here. If over 4 feet, it is pretty high and Bull Falls will be dangerous.

OTHER STREAMS IN THE MAIN STEM OF THE POTOMAC BASIN

LITTLE CACAPON RIVER: Frenchburg to Little Cacapon—24 Miles

MAPS: USGS—Levels, Largent, and Paw Paw
        COUNTY—Hampshire

Attractive run through quiet valley. The first 3 miles are almost continuous riffles over gravel and small ledges. The remainder of the run is slower. The scenery is mostly of a fairly narrow rural valley, but the last several miles appear remote and beautiful with nice wooded slopes which create an almost canyon-like atmosphere. High water is necessary to run from Frenchburg. Enough water at the start is plenty at the end.

TEARCOAT CREEK—3 Miles

MAPS: USGS—Hanging Rock
        COUNTY—Hampshire

This is a short but extremely beautiful run cutting across the red shaley grain of Hampshire County. It tumbles over an endless series of ledge rapids separated by short pools at the bottom of a shadowy lichen-covered gorge. US 50 is nearby but completely screened. It is a 3-mile run to North River.

NORTH RIVER—37 Miles

MAPS: USGS—Rio, Yellow Spring, Hanging Rock, Capon Bridge,
            and Largent
        COUNTY—Hampshire

This is a very small tributary of the Cacapon which is occasionally paddled when the water is very high elsewhere. It loops and winds through great curves for some 21 miles between US 50 and WV 127. Since the gradient is very little, the whitewater isn't very challenging except at the sharp turns, under low branches, etc. There are many fences, dangling wires, and branches to watch out for as well as a few log dams. A few miles above WV 127 is a 1.5-foot weir with a powerful roller. A large barn with a red silo is on the right. The most striking thing about this run is the access it provides to Ice Mountain, another of the Panhandle's incredible wonders. About 13 miles from the put-in, where the stream transcribes a sharp left-hand turn and is pinched in by steep rockslides to each side, you can find a place to stop and climb this freak of nature. Even in late summer, ice may be found beneath rocks and in crevices high on this natural refrigerator. When the river is very high the run on the far upper river, starting at the confluence of Grassy Lick Run on down about 3 miles to Rio, is nonstop action over boulders, ledges, and gravel. There are few eddies. At and below Rio are some interesting ledges, one of which has a very powerful keeper hydraulic.

SLEEPY CREEK: Smith Crossroads to Potomac River—19 Miles

MAPS: USGS—Stotlers Cross Roads and Cherry Run
         COUNTY—Morgan

This is the most beautiful of the 4 streams in the Eastern Panhandle. It has been run from the Virginia line, but normally paddlers prefer to put in at Smith Crossroads. This stream is at first fairly smooth, but starting about 3 miles above WV 9 it is graced with numerous riffles and small rapids (Class 1). About 2 miles below the start, not far below the low-water bridge at Johnsons Mill, the river turns hard left and plunges about 6 feet over a natural dam into a big round pool. Novices should carry because the hole at the bottom could be dangerous. The scenery from Johnsons Mill to the Potomac is extremely beautiful as the creek flows mostly through woodlands, past pretty bluffs and striking red shale cliffs and rock formations. In wet weather little falls decorate some of the cliffs. Take out above the Potomac at the village of Sleepy Creek. Access at WV 9 is heavily posted so ask permission. This is strictly a wet weather run.

BACK CREEK: WV 45 to WV 9—22 Miles

MAPS: USGS—Tablers Station and Big Pool
         COUNTY—Berkeley

This is a pretty run winding up the middle of Berkeley County. It flows through both woodlands and pastureland with good views of North Mountain to the east. Low-water bridges near Jones Springs and Tomahawk have adequate clearance at moderate levels, but the first one has much debris jammed against it and may require a carry.

Intermediate access can be made at a ford east of Ganotown, a bridge east of Shanghai, a bridge east of Jones Springs, or 2 bridges east of Tomahawk. There is no gauge, but enough water to cleanly run the riffle under WV 45 on the left is minimal yet adequate.

BACK CREEK: WV 9 to Potomac River—9 Miles

MAPS: USGS—Big Pool
          COUNTY—Berkeley

After passing a long line of summer homes, the creek loses itself in mostly remote woods. There are some fairly long, easy rapids (Class 1.5), especially below the first railroad bridge. There are also some pretty shale cliffs. There is a low-water bridge at Allensville Road which should be carried. It will scrape if run at most levels. This is the last take-out on Back Creek. The next take-out in West Virginia is at the upstream end of Little Georgetown, located about 4 miles down the Potomac.

OPEQUON CREEK: VA 672 (Wadesville) to WV 51—8 Miles

MAPS: USGS—Stephenson, Inwood, and Middle Way
          COUNTIES—Berkeley, Frederick, Va., and Clarke, Va.

This is a small stream meandering through a pretty, sparsely populated pastoral valley. Unfortunately, high banks often block much of any view of the scenery, save the many big, wonderful old farmhouses. The stream is mostly flat but swift with many very small riffles formed by fine gravel. The weather has to be fairly wet to run this. A minimal but adequate level would be about 3.2 feet on the Front Royal, Va. gauge.

OPEQUON CREEK: WV 51 to Potomac River—27 Miles

MAPS: USGS—Middle Way, Martinsburg, and Hedgesville
          COUNTIES—Berkeley and Jefferson

Not as pretty a section as that above. The first few miles have many summer homes and high banks hide the scenery. Noise from roads, an airport, and railroads is hard to escape. The creek is generally smooth, but there are a few riffles and a good current. A secondary road bridge on "12/7" provides an easy take-out about 200 yards above the mouth. A Front Royal gauge reading of 3.9 feet translates to about a foot on this section.

2 The Big Mountain River— The Mighty Cheat

The Cheat watershed is fantastic no matter which way you look at it. If you are a gung ho Corps of Engineers type, you drool in frustration at seeing water running freely every second over one of the largest uncontrolled watersheds in the East, but if you are a paddler you see it as a place with an almost infinite variety of water on which to test your skill and your boat. If you are an outdoors buff you are struck by the realization that the water you see high on Bald Knob when traveling on the Cass Scenic Railroad, the water you see pouring off Spruce Knob through the mountain hamlets of Job and Whitmer, the water you see plunging over Blackwater Falls, and the water you see forming an enchanting Arnout Hyde photograph at Bruceton Mills, all eventually wind up in the same river, the mighty Cheat.

It begins in the real mountains of the state in the form of 4 big forks, Shavers, Glady, Laurel, and Dry, each separated from its neighbors by massive, high mountain ridges. Shavers Fork even begins by actually flowing on top of one of these ridges for many miles. In this country, the shuttles are as fascinating as the rivers. Although Shavers Fork is considered the main source of the Cheat, and indeed is sometimes simply called "Cheat," Dry Fork has more important tributaries —the fascinating Gandy Creek, a stream that goes *through* a mountain, enters near Whitmer; Red Creek, draining the unique Dolly Sods wilderness area, has its mouth below Harman, Laurel and Glady Fork, which are the jewels of the system; the fabulous Otter Creek, which is a stream entirely within a wilderness area, enters above Hendricks; and finally at Hendricks itself, the wild and raucous Blackwater merges with Dry Fork with such volume that it is now called Black Fork and which, in just a few miles, joins Shavers Fork in Parsons to form the Cheat.

Two more significant paddling tributaries enter the Cheat, Horseshoe Run near historic Saint George, and the Big Sandy in the middle of the Cheat Canyon near Masontown. The Cheat comes to an ignoble end when it merges with northern West Virginia's sewer, the Monongahela, at Point Marion, Pennsylvania.

All of the Cheat tributaries and the Cheat itself below Rowlesburg are characterized by steep gradients, continuous action, pure, clean water (the lower Cheat, Big Sandy, and Blackwater excepted by mine acid), and spectacular scenery in largely unsettled areas.

There are many primitive and developed camping areas along the rivers of the watershed. Along Shavers Fork in the Cheat Bridge area (FS 209), where "12" crosses Glady Fork, and at Jenningston on Dry Fork, one will find primitive camping areas. At the mouth of the Big Sandy, one will find an ideal campsite in a very wild setting. The Forest Service has excellent fee area campgrounds at Stuart Recreation Area on Shavers Fork which, unfortunately, are rarely open, and a more primitive area at nearby Bear Heaven. There is another Forest Service fee area right on Horseshoe Run. The wilderness areas mentioned, Dolly Sods and Otter Creek, have attained wilderness protection by the Forest Service under terms of the Eastern Wilderness Act. There are 2 state parks near the rivers, Blackwater Falls and Canaan Valley. All of the upper forks are good trout streams spoiled only by the siltation of the strippers' shovels. Horseshoe Run is also a good trout stream as is the Big Sandy in the Bruceton Mills area. The Cheat itself offers good bass fishing down to a few miles below Rowlesburg where outrageous mine drainage sterilizes the river. There are even trout in the Cheat from Parsons to Saint George.

The dam builders are everywhere, but only a few fairly inconsequential products of their activities as yet exist. Very low, but dangerous dams exist on Shavers Fork at the Bowden bridge and on Dry Fork just below Harman. A low power company dam near Albright on the Cheat and the Cheat Reservoir power company dam near the state line are the only others, but these latter 2 are in areas of little interest to the paddler. The Corps wants to put in a huge dam at Rowlesburg on the Cheat which would undoubtedly improve Cheat Canyon and Narrows paddling all year around for the expert paddler, but this book is for all types of paddlers and the dam would spoil the entire Cheat Valley between Rowlesburg and Parsons. This valley is rich in history and beauty and is the major source of revenue for lovely Tucker County. At the present time, a power company is planning to dam up the upper Blackwater River, a very small stream and series of beaver ponds rarely paddled. The Corps and power companies have thoroughly studied the construction of impoundments on every single stream mentioned above. Those interested in what such impoundments would look like are urged to visit either the Cheat or Tygart reservoirs, 2 very large silt-catching basins of very low pH.

Recounting the history of the Cheat watershed would be the subject of a book in itself. The railroad and early logging days buff will nod in recognition as he paddles by the sites of the old logging towns along the rivers, like Spruce, Evenwood, Gladwin, Jenningston, Laneville, and many others. Some towns still exist today in the form of "bear camp" towns, like Bemis, while some have returned to dust, like the wild and woolly Brooklyn Heights were a dollar would buy you anything, and which is now known only as "a place across the river from Hendricks." The peaceful, outward calm of the mountain hamlets of Job and Whitmer belie their lawless past when murder, lynching, and robbery were the rule. No town has such interesting history as does Saint George, destined to be buried by a Corps of Engineers reservoir. Dating from the Revolution, changing sides many times during the Civil War, having its title of county seat and its records forcibly stolen and removed to Parsons by an outlaw army, this lovely little town, which has been repeatedly saved by the pluck of its people, seems doomed forever. George Washington knew of the lower Cheat and Big Sandy by exploring those parts near Morgantown for purposes of finding a waterway from the Potomac to the Ohio. George was told by ill-informed locals that the Cheat was navigable upstream for miles and wasn't too far from the equally navigable Potomac headwaters (the North Branch). It is a good thing George didn't try it! In fact, it is doubtful if our present leaders and policymakers get any better advice than this even today.

Logging is still a principal industry in the upper Cheat watershed, although the logs are not floated to downstream mills anymore. Agriculture does not flourish in such rugged terrain and is limited mostly to high mountain hay farms except for fertile farms along the Cheat below Parsons and certain places in Preston County. The latter is noted for its production of much of America's buckwheat, a product celebrated annually in Kingwood in September. Strip mining is becoming more popular and the results of this are far too evident to the paddler. Primarily, the Cheat watershed is encompassed by Monongahela National Forest, a playground of vast natural and scenic attraction. The tourist potential of this area is great if planned wisely.

Wildlife flourishes in this Cheat basin. Several black bear breeding areas are found. Deer and turkey are plentiful, but not as much as in the Eastern Panhandle. Some species are limited entirely to this area, e.g., the Cheat Mountain salamander. In other places several closely related species exist together, which is highly unusual, e.g., the 22 species of warblers that live on Gaudineer Knob on upper Shavers Fork. The uppermost reaches of the Cheat forks contain native brook trout, although their days are numbered if strip mining and clear cutting continue at the present rate. Beaver, muskrat, and occasional fishers might be seen. The high country is also a botanist's delight, whether his prize be the highly aromatic ramp or rare orchids. Balsam fir exists in several stands in the Cheat basin, and American larch makes it southernmost stronghold near the head of the Cheat Canyon at Cranesville.

Cheat River Canyon

Photograph courtesy of C. M. Laffey, Appalachian Wildwaters.

DRY FORK OF CHEAT RIVER

A. Dry Fork Above Gandy Creek—2+ Miles

MAPS: USGS—Whitmer
         Monongahela National Forest
         COUNTY—Randolph

This stream is nestled snugly between Rich and Allegheny mountains but has its source high up on Rich. The river is very small and exceedingly steep, but it follows the Spruce Knob road very closely. In periods of high runoff following the spring melts, this stream could conceivably be run for quite a distance above the mouth of Gandy Creek with but a few carries. It would be a continuous Class 2 chute. The river is very high and the weather up there becomes exceedingly severe. The scenery is magnificently rugged.

B. Gandy Creek to Wayside Park (WV 32)—12 Miles

CLASS	GRADIENT	VOLUME	SCENERY	TIME	LEVEL
1–3	40	S	B	4	0–2′

MAPS: USGS—Whitmer and Harman
         Monongahela National Forest
         COUNTY—Randolph

DESCRIPTION: This is a tremendously picturesque little stream winding through an immense, high mountain valley that reminds one of Switzerland. When viewed from US 33 off Rich Mountain, the result is fantastic. The stream tumbles continuously at a Class 1–2 pace from the mouth of Gandy Creek through a series of highland meadow farms until the US 33 bridge is reached. There are no difficulties in this upper section unless a fallen tree or log temporarily dams the stream.

DIFFICULTIES: After passing under the US 33 bridge, the stream begins to get more difficult. Several ledges are encountered and a wooden dam just below Harman can be run, but scout to avoid the middle piling. From Harman to the take-out, the stream returns to its continuous Class 2 character with 2 Class 3 rapids in the last half mile.

SHUTTLE: The put-in may be reached from US 33 by taking "29" south just upstream from the bridge. Continue through Job to the next fork. A put-in can be made on either Gandy Creek or Dry Fork at bridges just upstream from the fork. The take-out is located 2 miles north of Harman on WV 32 at the Wayside Park.

GAUGE: There is a canoeing gauge under the US 33 bridge. Also, inspection of the low ledges below this bridge should tell you whether there is enough water. When the Parsons gauge (see other sections) is greater than 5, consider the run possible.

C. WV 32 to Jenningston—7 Miles

CLASS	GRADIENT	VOLUME	SCENERY	TIME	LEVEL
2	36	S	A–B	2	0.5'

MAPS: USGS—Harman and Mozark Mountain
Monongahela National Forest
COUNTIES—Tucker and Randolph

DESCRIPTION: This is a charming run lazily meandering through scenic farmland, rich in history from the boom days of logging. As one approaches Jenningston, more isolated parts of the forest are traversed, but even these are interrupted by the remains of old abandoned homesteads, schools, and churches, reminders of more populous times. The river is steady Class 2 with the intervening pools being short, thus providing almost continuous action. At higher water levels the waves and turbulence could easily become Class 3 in the lower stretches. The mouth of Laurel Fork about a half mile above Jenningston bridge is a beautiful spot and the turbulence of the stream makes a fun "playing around" rapids.

DIFFICULTIES: Other than an occasional overhanging branch or low swinging bridge, there are no difficulties. This would be an ideal stream for open boats if the water level were at 1 foot or more. No maneuvering would be involved. Try and catch this one when there is snow on the ground; it's beautiful.

SHUTTLE: Halfway between the villages of Dry Fork and Harman, a bridge crosses the stream from WV 32. Launch the boats from the small Wayside Park on the opposite side. Take out at the homemade picnic grounds on the left bank below the bridge in Jenningston.

Jenningston may be found by turning left at the first road past the village of Red Creek when traveling toward Parsons on WV 72. The river is 2 miles from this junction.

GAUGE: Right-hand, stream-side of bridge support in Jenningston. Also, since WV 32 is so close to the upper part of the stream, one can make a good visual inspection of the water level there. If you can canoe the first 50–100 yards from the put-in, you will have no trouble.

D. Jenningston to Hendricks — 12 Miles

CLASS	GRADIENT	VOLUME	SCENERY	TIME	LEVEL
3_4	25	723	A–B	4	0–2'

MAPS: USGS — Mozark Mountain
Monongahela National Forest
COUNTY — Tucker

DESCRIPTION: Although not as long as Shavers Fork, this tributary of the Cheat has a larger volume. This section of Dry Fork does not meander but proceeds directly northwest to Parsons through a rather deep trough. The scenery, although beautiful, is more pastoral than the other Cheat tributaries because signs of civilization are always present, such as quaint old homesteads, churches, rural schools, etc.

The rapids are fairly close together, providing rather continuous excitement. Many drop over ledges and the waves are large and heavy. One of the most enjoyable rivers in the state.

DIFFICULTIES: About 1 mile below the put-in the river divides. After the forks rejoin, a steep rapids veers off to the right and curves back to the left. The paddler is forced to the right. As he gets to the bottom, he must either scramble very quickly back to the far left or be prepared to blast through a big hydraulic at the bottom.

After passing under the second rickety swinging footbridge, things begin to pick up. About 400 yards below this bridge, there are a couple of steep riverwide hydraulics. These can be avoided by sticking to the far right side of the river.

The 2 rapids below the mouth of Otter Creek (marked by the third swinging footbridge) could offer difficulty. The first is a right-hand turn obstructed by large rocks, and care is needed to avoid broaching in the turn. The next rapids is probably the most difficult of the entire

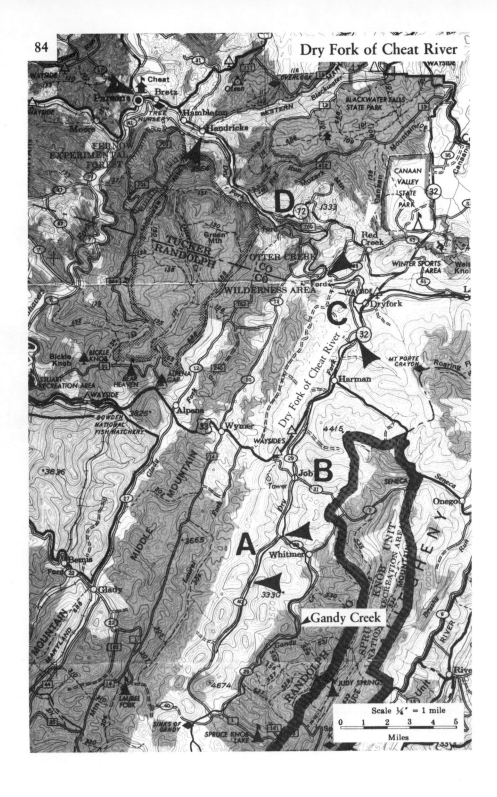

Gandy Creek

Scale ¼" = 1 mile

0 1 2 3 4 5

Miles

run. The approach is partly obscured by a bus-sized boulder on the left. One must make an S turn around this boulder beginning at the right and then immediately going back to the left and then over a drop through some fairly heavy and complicated water. Consider all of the rapids below the second swinging footbridge as Class 4 in high water.

SHUTTLE: This is very exciting! Hendricks is located on WV 72 which is a very narrow, tortuous road over high mountains and deep hollows. The scenery up there is superb among the high mountain meadows, but if you want to look, stop your car. You can take out just above the mouth of the Blackwater or upstream a half mile from Hendricks gauge off WV 72. A shorter trip with a simplified shuttle is to put in at Rich Ford on CR 26. CR 26 turns south off of WV 72 just east of Red Run. Proceed on CR 26 to the river. Jenningston can be reached via "35/16" near the village of Red Creek. If you come to this village from Parsons, you have passed the turn-off.

GAUGE: Downstream of the right-side abutment of the Jenningston bridge. One can call the Monongahela Power Company office in various northern West Virginia cities and ask for the dispatcher. He can give you the Cheat River reading below Parsons. Do not attempt if below 4 feet. The National Weather Service office in Pittsburgh can give the Parsons reading; call (412) 644-2890. There is also a government gauge at Hendricks which should be above 3 feet.

BLACK FORK OF THE CHEAT RIVER

Mouth of Blackwater River to Parsons Tannery—4 Miles

CLASS	GRADIENT	VOLUME	SCENERY	TIME	LEVEL
2–3	25	1,109	B	1	4–6′

MAPS: USGS—Mozark Mountain and Parsons
COUNTY—Tucker

DESCRIPTION: The Black Fork's name, like its water, is the contraction of the Blackwater and the Dry Fork rivers. Don't confuse it with its untamed shrew of a mother—the Blackwater—but consider it a chip off the old block—the Dry Fork. The Black Fork is an end-of-the-day type of trip, ideally topping off a lower Shavers Fork or Dry Fork trip. The river courses between wooded mountain ranges only partially spoiled by traces of civilization. It is an extension in scenery and type of water of its major parent, the Dry Fork. Little maneuvering is necessary, but the volume and gradient combine to provide a rocking-horse ride over 3-foot, uniform-standing waves.

SHUTTLE: Put in on the Blackwater River under the bridge at Hendricks and go down 400 yards of Class 3 rapids to the junction with Dry Fork. One can take out at the Parsons tannery (this is private land so permission should be secured), or extend the trip 2 miles by paddling down to the junction with Shavers Fork and on to the Holly Meadows bridge for a much more scenic take-out. This can be reached from WV 72 below Parsons by turning right on "1." (See maps for the Dry Fork of Cheat River, above.)

GAUGE: The above readings are for the Parsons gauge on the Cheat, (412) 644-2890. The Hendricks gauge can be read on the spot and should be over 2.2 feet.

GANDY CREEK

Sinks of Gandy Outlet to Dry Fork—13 Miles

CLASS	GRADIENT	VOLUME	SCENERY	TIME	LEVEL
2-3	37	S	A	2	4-5'

MAPS: USGS—Spruce Knob and Whitmer
Monongahela National Forest
COUNTY—Randolph

DESCRIPTION: Gandy Creek disappears in a high meadow on the west side of Spruce Knob, swallowed by a cave. A mile and a half away over the ridge, Gandy emerges as a whitewater stream. Only during flood periods is there enough volume for paddling, and then it's a sporty run. The most significant water is at a big diagonal stopper under a footbridge halfway down. There are 3-foot waves and holes along the road above Whitmer.

DIFFICULTIES: Like all little steep streams there is the constant danger of being pushed into barbed wire and steel cable fences, strained under log footbridges, and impaled on sturdy fallen tree branches. The paddler must be able to scramble for nonexistent eddies like a pro quarterback buying time for covered receivers.

SHUTTLE: Easy. Pick your section along "29" from Dry Fork to the Sinks exit. (See maps for the Dry Fork of Cheat River, above.)

GAUGE: When Randy Carter's gauge at the US 33 bridge on Dry Fork disappears, Gandy is up. This requires about 11 feet on the Cheat gauge at Parsons, (412) 644-2890.

RED CREEK

North Branch Bridge to WV 32—6 Miles

CLASS	GRADIENT	VOLUME	SCENERY	TIME	LEVEL
3–4	75	S	A	2	NA

MAPS: USGS—Laneville
      Monongahela National Forest
      COUNTIES—Tucker and Randolph

DESCRIPTION: This little river draining the Dolly Sods area is available only in very wet seasons. Put in at the bridge on the North Branch just above the confluence with the South Branch and be ready to maneuver because there will be no rest until the water seeping under your skirt dictates dumping. The river falls at a steady rate through the ghost lumbering town of Laneville, past the first footbridge and ford, and on to the second footbridge at the ancient Canaan Crossing. This second footbridge marks a section of low ledges and stoppers. The course continues with Mount Porte Crayon towering 2,500 feet on the left and Cabin Mountain on the right. Surprisingly soon, the WV 32 bridge appears. The river continues for a mile to join the Dry Fork of the Cheat. The most convenient take-out is a quarter mile upstream from the mouth at an old bridge.

DIFFICULTIES: The upper part of the river may be described as busy, while that below the low-water bridge at Laneville consists of bigger drops and waves. Approach the Laneville low-water bridge with caution and carry on the right. The first big ledge comes up fast at the end of an S turn. The smaller channels are often clogged by downed trees.

SHUTTLE: The put-in is reached by taking "45" east of WV 32 for 6 miles to the put-in bridge. If the water in the upper part appears too low, try an alternate put-in at the Laneville low-water bridge (also reachable via FS 19). The take-out bridge is on WV 32. (See maps for the Dry Fork of Cheat River, above.)

GAUGE: No gauge at present. Consider water at the bottom of the downstream drain on right abutment of WV 32 bridge as adequate.

LAUREL FORK

A. Laurel Fork Campground to US 33—16 Miles

CLASS	GRADIENT	VOLUME	SCENERY	TIME	LEVEL
1	21	S	A	5	1–2′

MAPS: USGS—Sinks of Gandy, Glady, Whitmer, and Harman
Monongahela National Forest
COUNTIES—Randolph

DESCRIPTION: The upper Laurel Fork is an intimate, easy stream that can float the canoe-camper almost back to the eighteenth century. Its availability is limited to periods of very high water in the winter and spring. Leaving the campground is the end of civilization for a day—a day of chasing deer and beaver along a swift-flowing river through marshy glades. The river is continuous fast water in a shallow narrow bed.

DIFFICULTIES: The paddler must be able to control his boat well enough to avoid being pushed into fallen and overhanging trees.

SHUTTLE: From the take-out at the US 33 bridge go west 1 mile and then south along the spine of Middle Mountain, on FS 14, for 12 miles, then left down to the Laurel Fork campground on the road to Spruce Knob.

GAUGE: The gauge is located on the right upstream side of the US 33 bridge. Do not expect it to be up unless the Parsons gauge on Cheat is over 7 feet; call (412) 644-2890 to get a reading of the Parsons gauge.

B. US 33 to Jenningston—13 Miles

CLASS	GRADIENT	VOLUME	SCENERY	TIME	LEVEL
3–4	9@71	S	A	5	0.3–1.5′

MAPS: USGS—Harman
Monongahela National Forest
COUNTIES—Randolph and Tucker

DESCRIPTION: This is unquestionably the best run of the Cheat basin, all things considered. It is a long trip through uninhabited and

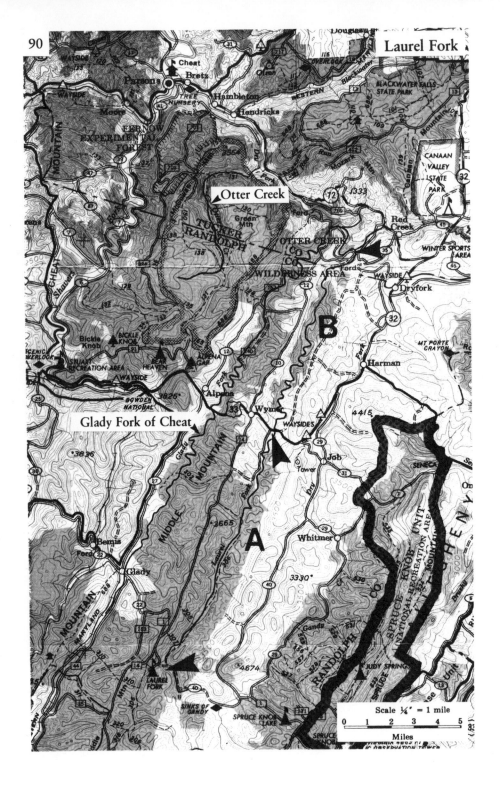

Otter Creek

Glady Fork of Cheat

Scale ¼" = 1 mile

0   1   2   3   4   5

Miles

virtually inaccessible country in the high valley between the Middle and Rich mountains. The remnants of an early logging railroad play tag with the meandering river for the first 3.6 miles, crossing it 4 times on the artifacts of disappeared bridges. At this point, one hour into the trip, you encounter the first of a series of 2- to 4-foot ledges. These continue regularly for the next 2 miles to the granddaddy of them all, a 12-foot runnable waterfall which you should portage on the left along the tramway bed. After lunch at the foot of the falls, be ready for 7 miles of continuous Class 3 rapids to the mouth. There are a total of 8 bridge crossings on the run. None of the bridges remain but the abutments are readily spotted as landmarks. Between the seventh and eighth bridges there is a 50-yard tunnel from one limb of a half-mile loop to the other. The water visible at the mouth is typical of the entire river from the falls down. This is a very exhilarating run amidst the least spoiled scenery of West Virginia. After being flushed out into the Dry Fork, it is just a quarter mile to the Jenningston bridge.

DIFFICULTIES: Spotting the falls from upstream should be no problem. It takes about 1.5 hours of paddling time to reach the falls. There are 6 bridge crossings to the falls; the sixth one is about a mile above the falls. The falls are just around a right turn. Fluorescent strips have been tied in the tree branches on the left above the falls. The only other difficulty is the fatigue of 13 miles of wilderness travel, including 9 miles of continuous maneuvering.

SHUTTLE: The put-in is at the US 33 bridge. The take-out is at the mouth downstream along the left side from the Jenningston bridge. The best way between the 2 points is west along US 33, 4 miles to Alpena, and north on "12" by the Glady Fork and Sully.

GAUGE: There is a gauge painted on the right-side abutment of the US 33 bridge. It will not be high enough unless the Parsons gauge is over 5 feet.

GLADY FORK OF CHEAT RIVER

US 33 Bridge to Mouth on Dry Fork (Gladwin)—16.5 Miles

CLASS	GRADIENT	VOLUME	SCENERY	TIME	LEVEL
	9@33				
1–3	7.5@46	S	A	5–6	0.5–2′

MAPS: USGS—Bowden, Harman, and Mozark Mountain
      Monongahela National Forest
      COUNTIES—Randolph and Tucker

DESCRIPTION: There are very few flat pools anywhere on this small, meandering stream. The rapids are continuous but not difficult. The upper river is very shallow, but when it is full, turns must be precise. Fallen tree hazards across the smaller channels are a real problem and caution is urged. The novice should be able to make a good eddy turn.

Below the bridge to Sully (mile 9) the current keeps up a steady Class 2 pace, but soon the gradient begins to pick up. The last 3 or 4 miles are considerably more interesting as the waves, hydraulics, and passages become greater and more complex. The entire run is in a beautiful wilderness setting. Do not get too close to the low-water bridge at the take-out because the current is very powerful under it.

SHUTTLE: Put in at the US 33 bridge. A take-out for a 9-mile trip may be had by taking "12" north out of Alpena and parking at the bridge. There is excellent camping here or along the road to the left before the bridge. From the bridge to Gladwin is another 7.5 river miles. Continue on "12" taking a left at each of the next 2 forks. At the bottom of the very steep hill, turn left again and cross the low-water bridge, the take-out. It is possible to extend this trip by continuing on this road over the hill until it dead-ends at Dry Fork. The paddler could carry the bridge, continue down to the mouth, and paddle down Dry Fork 3 miles to the car. (See Laurel Fork map, above.)

GAUGE: There is a gauge on the Sully bridge. Also, the water should be at least 6 inches over the drain pipe on the right abutment of the US 33 bridge. You will need at least 5 feet on the Parsons gauge; call (412) 644-2890.

OTTER CREEK

Big Springs Gap to Dry Fork—2.6 Miles

CLASS	GRADIENT	VOLUME	SCENERY	TIME	LEVEL
4	101	S	A	2	4.5–5'

MAPS: USGS—Mozark Mountain
Monongahela National Forest
COUNTY—Tucker

DESCRIPTION: Otter Creek flows out of a roadless wilderness range of black bear, turkeys, and backpackers. It is little and steep and hard to get to. One must be determined to paddle it to catch it at the right level. Otter Creek should be scouted from the old water-level logging tramway trail along its entire length even if the paddler never catches it at the right level for a run. The headwaters can be reached from Alpena Gap off US 33. There is a service road to a series of limestone-filled tumbling drums which the state maintains as an experiment in trying to neutralize the naturally acid stream and improve its potential as a native trout stream. From there to Big Springs Gap it quadruples its volume as it meanders through a marsh area for 4 miles and then cascades at a steady 200 fpm for 4 more miles. Only at Big Springs Gap does it become reasonably boatable.

From the Big Springs Gap put-in to the mouth there is no rest. It is hard work to find an eddy in which to catch one's breath. The creek is continuous, requires quick maneuvering in a small boulder patch, and contains irregularly placed large boulders with hydraulics, pinning possibilities, and some downstream blind spots. Scouting Otter Creek is like trying to plan a course down a bobsled run. It's very exhilarating but also very tiring.

DIFFICULTIES: About a half mile into the trip there is a cross-stream log on a ledge that will need to be carried. More logs could appear, so be ready to eddy out, preferably on the right side since the trail is there. The left side is steep and choked with laurel.

SHUTTLE: Set up the take-out at the Hendricks gauge for a fast 2.5 mile finish down the Dry Fork from Otter Creek's mouth. Shuttle back into Parsons and follow signs to Fernow Experimental Forest.

Park at Big Springs Gap trail and carry 20 minutes down the trail to the put-in. (See Laurel Fork map, above.)

GAUGE: There is a gauge at the mouth of Otter Creek which can be surveyed by taking a short walk from WV 72. The Cheat gauge at Parsons will be in the 7- to 10-foot range when Otter Creek is up. The Hendricks gauge on Dry Fork should be at about 5 feet.

Ward Eister on the Blackwater River

BLACKWATER RIVER

A. CR 35/18 near Cortland to Davis—11 Miles

CLASS	GRADIENT	VOLUME	SCENERY	TIME	LEVEL
A–3	9	193	A	4	3–4.5'

MAPS: USGS—Blackwater Falls and Davis
Monongahela National Forest
COUNTY—Tucker

DESCRIPTION: Appalachian Power wants this river. They wish to "enhance" the beauty of the Land of Canaan by flooding it. Until they do, this is a unique highland marsh drained by the Blackwater and its dendritic tributaries. The river is flat but swift with clear brown ("black") water. Signs of beaver business highlight the trip. The character of the river changes when it passes through the gap in Brown Mountain. The last couple of miles are enjoyable ledges. The trip ends in the pool of a 10-foot dam at Davis.

SHUTTLE: To reach the put-in, take "35" south of WV 32 3 miles to the bridge over North Branch. Turn toward the east. A gate blocks the road in a half mile. Carry one quarter mile to the river. Take out at Davis.

GAUGE: There is a gauge at Davis, but there is no place to call to get a reading. The pertinent numbers are the ones given above. A general index is that the Parsons gauge on Cheat should be over 5 feet.

B. North Fork Junction to Hendricks—7 Miles

CLASS	GRADIENT	VOLUME	SCENERY	TIME	LEVEL
4_6	5@112	193	A	4	2.5–3.5'

MAPS: USGS—Mozark Mountain
Monongahela National Forest
COUNTY—Tucker

DESCRIPTION: This is West Virginia's longest continuous rapids. It flows through a narrow, steep defile draining the Canaan Valley. The valley is a flat upland swamp on the west side of the Allegheny Front.

Multiple branches of the upper Blackwater funnel the 150-square-mile drainage basin into 2 main forks which respectively pass the former logging capitals of Davis and Thomas. Near these nineteenth-century towns, they suddenly leap off the mountain as 2 falls, 50 feet each, and begin their unrelenting rush to the Dry Fork 8 miles and 1,000 feet below. The 2 main divisions of the river, the Blackwater and its North Fork, confluence about a mile below their initiation drops and slow their descent to a more "realistic" paddling gradient. Both falls, the one preserved by a state park and the other on the North Branch, should be viewed by the paddler.

From the recommended put-in at the junction and with only minimal veering from left or right, the river is 1 continuous blind bend—downwards. From the paddler's eye level he can never see more than 50 yards to where the river disappears over the edge of the world. It has a fantastic 112 fpm gradient for 5 miles to Lime Rock, an abandoned community 2 miles upstream from Hendricks. Fortunately, this descent is not broken into alternate stretches of rapids and pools but is evenly distributed. It is a gigantic sluiceway between mountains rising 2,000 feet on either side with almost no riverside bench.

Paddling the Blackwater is a constant challenge of reading and negotiating chutes over staircase ledges randomly strewn with 5- to 10-foot boulders. The paddler is constantly maneuvering in the ever-pushing current. Moving side eddies are the only rest or rescue spots along the course. The waters of the river are a nonsilted brown covered with suds—a form of pollution that has been noted since the time of Thomas Lewis, a 1746 explorer who appropriately called this stream "the River Styx." The color is attributed to organic acids from the upland swamps leaching iron oxides from the red shale that lines much of the riverbed.

In the first 1.5 miles, there is a unique rapids that serves as a landmark. The water races 75 yards over a flat, sloping red shale floor. With this minimization of friction, the current reaches horrendous speeds before abruptly dropping into a giant washing machine at the bottom. Shortly below this is Tub Run, a tributary on the right.

The last 2 miles into Hendricks drop at an interesting 48 fpm and could be run separately beginning at Lime Rock. The trail to Lime Rock is accessible with permission from the Hinchcliff Lumber Company at Hendricks on weekdays only and at the risk of traversing a very marginal looking log-and-plank bridge.

The Blackwater has been run from the base of Blackwater Falls to the North Fork, but that's a trip only for those heavily into self-punishment. Many rapids have to be carried making the run really a test of rhododendron thicket vs. kayaker. It is an understatement that we cannot recommend it.

DIFFICULTIES: To single out any part of this trip as difficult is ludicrous. Everything about it, from getting to the put-in to the take-out, is difficult beyond the scope of all but the expert paddler. While the river is mostly Class 3, the overall series without pools and the inevitable fatigue of constant maneuvering make this a Class 4 run. Another complication to consider is that the river runs in a south-westerly direction against the afternoon sun.

Approximately 200 yards downstream from the put-in are 2 closely spaced drops that are Class 6 at most water levels. The first has a horrible hole and the second a very tight channel into an undercut rock. Both may be carried at the same time down the left bank. The next several drops are blind from the top and have inconsiderately placed rocks at the bottom of the main drops, so scout if you cannot see from the boat. There is always the danger of tree strainers in these rapids. Soon thereafter, the slide rapids is encountered.

About halfway through the trip, a shallow, wide, 8- to 10-foot falls is found which may be carried or scraped over on the left. Paddle across the pool and look at the next rapids below as the river now funnels into a huge hole. Most people choose to carry this also.

SHUTTLE: The shuttle is easy, but the put-in is a bear. From the take-out under the WV 72 bridge in Hendricks, take US 219 to Thomas, and then right to Coketon, and on to Douglas via "27." Park where the road leaves the river, shoulder your boat, and walk 1 mile. That's right—1 mile along railroad track, then slide it down 250 feet over a wooded 60-degree incline to the river. Incidentally, the railroad parallels the river some 300 feet above the water and serves as an avenue back to civilization in case of accidents.

GAUGE: The above gauge readings refer to the Davis gauge. See section A, above. A paddler's gauge on the Hendricks bridge may be meaningless since someone has been reworking the riverbed with a bulldozer. If the river looks scrapy from the bridge, it is probably adequate. If it looks adequate, it is probably too high. The Parsons gauge rule of thumb for the run is 4–5.5 feet.

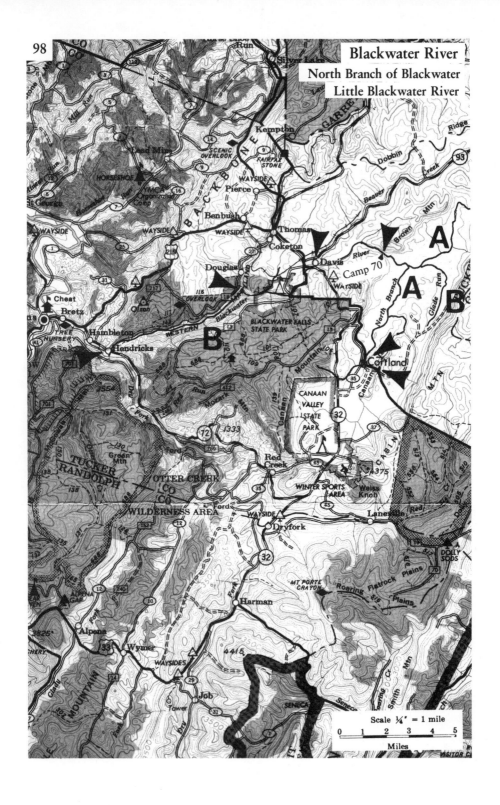

Scale ¼" = 1 mile

0 1 2 3 4 5

Miles

NORTH BRANCH OF BLACKWATER RIVER

Cortland to Camp 70—9 Miles

CLASS	GRADIENT	VOLUME	SCENERY	TIME	LEVEL
A	3	NA	A	4	NA

MAPS: USGS—Blackwater Falls and Davis
 Monongahela National Forest
 COUNTY—Tucker

DESCRIPTION: The North Branch is eminently runnable at times when the Blackwater paralleling it is only a trickle over the shale. Don't be discouraged by the unrunnable riffle at the bridge and the narrowness of the stream; it is deep enough and gradually widens. About ¾ mile from the start, alders crowd the stream for a quarter mile, but beyond, the depth increases and the only obstacles are occasional beaver dams. The last mile before the Blackwater, the North Branch snakes across broad beaver meadows. After 3.5 miles on the North Branch, the first take-out is 5.5 miles down the Blackwater at Camp 70. The scenery on the Blackwater will seem anticlimactic.

SHUTTLE: Take "35" south from WV 32 to Cortland for the put-in, 700 feet east, below the fence and bridge. For the take-out, go north on WV 32 to Davis, cross the Blackwater, and make the first right. Cross Beaver Creek on an old railroad bridge (it's safe in spite of the sign) and follow the dirt road 4 miles to Camp 70. If the Blackwater is up, a take-out at Yellow Creek eliminates the roughest part of the road. Whitewater paddlers could of course take out at Davis.

 A trip requiring no shuttle would be to paddle down the Blackwater from Cortland and return up the North Branch, which is easily ascended, for a 7-mile circuit. (See the map for Blackwater River, above.)

GAUGE: If the first half mile is even marginally runnable, there will be plenty of water for the rest of the trip. In a normal year, the river is runnable all spring and occasionally in other seasons. This is due not only to the low gradient and bogs but also to the geologic structure. About 1.5 miles below Freeland Run, the Blackwater leaves the Greenbrier limestone to enter a shale ridge. Just over a mile north in the same limestone layer is the North Branch, 40 feet lower. Some of the mainstream's water is pirated underground to Cortland.

LITTLE BLACKWATER RIVER

A. Camp 72 to Camp 70 (Blackwater River)—6 Miles

CLASS	GRADIENT	VOLUME	SCENERY	TIME	LEVEL
A	5	NA	A	Varies	NA

MAPS: USGS—Davis and Mount Storm Lake
Monongahela National Forest
COUNTY—Tucker

DESCRIPTION: The Little Blackwater winds down the center of the wildest part of Canaan Valley. Treeless and windswept, the dark river offers panoramic vistas of vast bogs, island meadows, and the encircling mountains that make the valley unique.

The stream meanders incessantly, dropping over many little beaver dams, but has only 1 tree across it.

SHUTTLE: None. The best approach is to paddle up the Little Blackwater from the Forks at Blackwater River. The nearest start is Camp 70. The low gradient and lack of rapids make for easy upriver travel. Turn left on the Little Blackwater after 1¾ miles. For those determined to never go upriver, a rough jeep road leads down to Camp 72 from a jeep road along Cabin Mountain.

GAUGE: None. The stream is normally runnable to Camp 72 all spring and for 1.5 miles above the Forks in June. The river is still runnable above Camp 72, but no one has yet ascended so far.

B. Glade Run of the Little Blackwater—3 Miles

CLASS	GRADIENT	VOLUME	SCENERY	TIME	LEVEL
A	5	NA	A+	Varies	NA

MAPS: USGS—Davis and Mount Storm Lake
Monongahela National Forest
COUNTY—Tucker

DESCRIPTION: Tiny, shallow Glade Run is the most scenic of all Canaan Valley streams. The section described here begins where a narrow logging railroad once bridged the stream. Bumping against the base of Cabin Mountain, it wanders north across beaver meadows. It is narrow, deep, and drinkable. Soon Glade Run swings northwest across the valley along the end of a low shale ridge. There is a beaver dam made of small, flat plates of shale stacked up and topped with a bit of brush. (See map for Blackwater River, above.)

SHUTTLE: None. Definitely an upriver trip. Just go up as far as you care to and coast back down. Put in at Camp 70, paddle up the Blackwater 1¾ miles, left on the Little Blackwater, and then after about 1 mile, right on Glade Run.

GAUGE: None. Runnable within several days of rain or snowmelt in April and May. The midsection on shale is the limiting factor.

SHAVERS FORK OF CHEAT RIVER

A. Spruce to Cheat Bridge—17 Miles

CLASS	GRADIENT	VOLUME	SCENERY	TIME	LEVEL
1–2	18	S	A	6	NA

MAPS: USGS—Cass, Snyder Knob, and Durbin
Monongahela National Forest
COUNTIES—Randolph and Pocahontas

DESCRIPTION: The put-in is at 3,900 feet, making it probably the highest run in the East. Here the river is very narrow and fast with mostly Class 2 rapids. There are many easy (Class 1 and 2) rapids and many pools. Your first landmarks are 2 railroad trestles a few hundred yards apart (Twin Bridges). In another half mile, Rocky Run, or "Rocky Ridge Run," enters from the left. In another 2 miles, you will pass under a third trestle and then be joined by the Second Fork of Shavers from the right (known as Big Run among the locals). The bridge marks the end of the best action—the first 5 miles have 32 fpm gradient. The river then broadens out a bit but still moves pretty fast. The rapids are Class 1–2, with the 2's occurring at sharp bends. We did not see any particularly hazardous or difficult spots anywhere.

Other significant tributaries enter the stream from the left at roughly miles 8 (Beaver Creek), 9 (Buck Run), and 10 (Black Run). The road comes very close to the river at several points between these latter 2 runs, making access from Cheat Bridge easy. This part would make a splendid open-boat fishing trip. The gradient averages 18–14 fpm and finally drops to only 10. The fourth bridge marks mile 12. From here down to Cheat Bridge, the river is very wide and shallow with very few riffles, which are Class 1 and occur at constrictions and bends in the river. The entire run is a 17-mile trip through exquisite scenery. The regenerating spruce forest, the bogs, and mountain meadows remind one of Canada.

SHUTTLE: Your first problem is setting up the shuttle and getting in to Spruce. Two private roads (Mower Lumber Co.) exist, but experience has shown that they might be snowbound when you want in. When the roads are clear, the water might be too low. (On the other hand, there may be potential for access from the Snowshoe Ski Area.)

We recommend that you commence your shuttle at Cheat Bridge near US 250. Turn right on Red Run Road just east of the river and continue upriver through the extinct town of Cheat Bridge. Don't cross the iron bridge, but stay on the upstream left all of the way. Please note: To use the Mower Lumber Co. road, a permit must be obtained in advance. Write to Mower Lumber Co., Box 27, Durbin, WV 26264 and state when you will want to use the road; there is a small daily fee.

GAUGE: The only known run of the entire section was made at a level of exactly 9 stones down from the top on the left abutment of the iron bridge above US 250. This level was adequate but occasionally scrapy in the first mile.

B. US 250 to McGee Run—10.5 Miles

CLASS	GRADIENT	VOLUME	SCENERY	TIME	LEVEL
1–2$_3$	21 (2@32)	S	A	3	NA

MAPS: USGS—Durbin and Wildell
Monongahela National Forest
COUNTY—Randolph

DESCRIPTION: This is a very pleasant run on a beautiful river, one of the finest in the state, but also the one in the most jeopardy from industrialization. No stream in the state receives as many or as big individual fish from the state's trout-stocking program. Indeed, the last 5.5-mile section has been designated a Fish-for-Fun stream, where angling is limited to barbless hooks and all trout must be returned. This is where you will find the expert fishermen in the state. The river is flanked by spruce, hemlock, and even balsam. The wildlife is fantastic, especially the birds. The run is very easy down to Water Tank Run which enters from the right through large culverts. (If you want to keep track, the names of the runs that you will pass in order from the put-in are Red Run, Stonecoal, Whitmeadow from the left, Glade and John's Camp from the right, Crouch from the left, then Water Tank, and finally Yokum and McGee from the left.)

DIFFICULTIES: At Water Tank, the river becomes steeper and the rapids more or less continuous although only Class 2. There are 3 pretty nice drops—1 just below Glade Run, 1 right at Yokum, and 1 more before the take-out. Just upstream from the mouth of Yokum, the paddler will pass under the bridge and coal conveyor of the con-

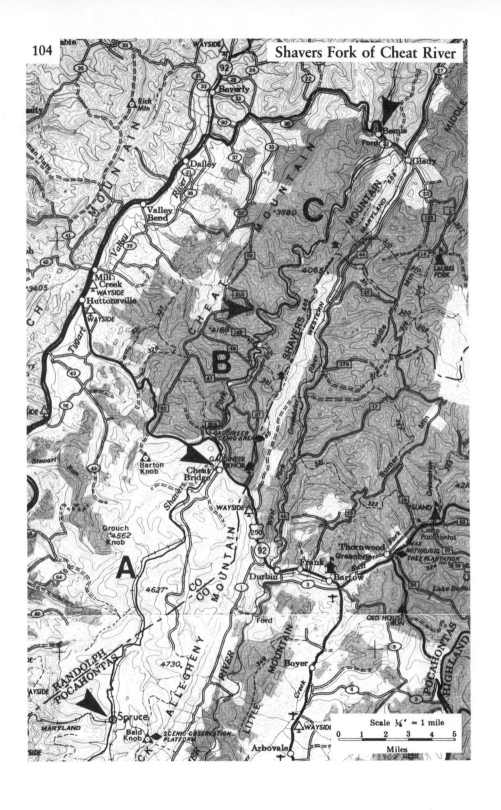

troversial Linan Mines. There has been considerable question about whether an industrial development like this can coexist with a beautiful, near-wilderness trout stream. If not, anglers and whitewater paddlers will be the first to know in the future.

SHUTTLE: Put in at the US 250 bridge. To reach the take-out, head back west along this highway and take the second road to the right, FS 92. From this Forest Service road there are many side roads that lead down to Shavers Fork along some of the runs named above. Not all of these roads are passable. Continue on FS 92 to the end and turn right down the hollow of McGee Run. There is a primitive campground at the end of the Fish-for-Fun section.

GAUGE: None at present. If you can paddle around at the put-in bridge without scraping, you will be OK. You will need at least 1.5 feet at CR 33/8 gauge (see section E, below).

C. McGee Run to Bemis—13 Miles

CLASS	GRADIENT	VOLUME	SCENERY	TIME	LEVEL
$3-5_6$	58	544	A	6	1-2'

MAPS: USGS—Wildell, Beverly East, and Glady
          Monongahela National Forest
          COUNTY—Randolph

DESCRIPTION: After the longest shuttle in the state, the longest access paddle in the state, and carrying the most spectacular falls in the state, then you can pit your paddling skill and strength against 4 miles of the wildest water tumbling over 6 more falls, one of which is Class 6, and with no slack water between the drops.

The first part is wide and shallow at reasonable water levels, but it soon picks up speed slipping down over sloping rocks. A landmark at 5 miles is a railroad marker visible from the river marked C-7; a mile later, C-6; and at 7.5 miles, R/S is marked in green. Other than watching for these railroad signs, little else characterizes the first 3 hours of the trip except isolated wilderness.

Shortly after the last railroad marker, there is an ominous-looking blind rapids on a sharp right turn, but it is safe to run. The High Falls of Cheat will be met at mile 9, a riverwide abrupt drop of 15 feet, one of the most spectacular sights in West Virginia. It is a clean drop for those who enjoy falls-dropping. There is a beautiful primitive campsite

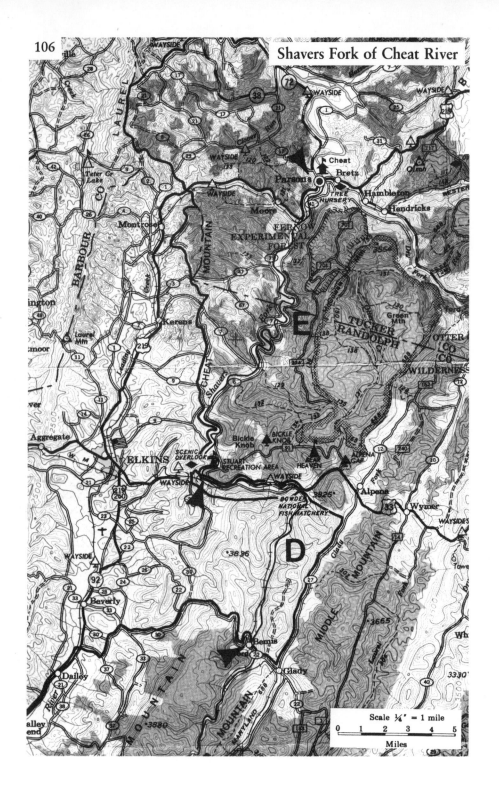

Scale ¼" = 1 mile

0 1 2 3 4 5

Miles

on the right used by backpackers. This is located at the mouth of Fall Run on the county map or Red Run on the topo.

DIFFICULTIES: One-half mile below the High Falls is a Class 6 runnable falls. This complex consists of several ledges at the top and a thundering, slanting, right-to-left canted, 6-foot drop. There is a large boulder immediately in the center run-out and jagged rocks in the ledge on the left. It is doubtful if one could keep to the right because of the diagonal shape of the ledge. It is a Class 6 because of the pinning possibility on the bottom boulder. The carry is easy on the right by lowering one's boat over the rock and climbing down.

Below this adrenaline-pumping obstruction, the paddler has finally arrived at what this trip is all about. There is continuous Class 4 whitewater for 3.5 miles to Bemis. You get a bit too busy to look for landmarks, but it is hard to miss the 2 railroad bridges at 11 and 11.3 miles. The second bridge is at the site of a runnable, sharp-dropping 6-foot falls, which should be scouted at higher levels. In the last 2 miles there are more 4- to 5-foot ledges, all runnable.

To sum up then, there is first the High Falls which are easy to recognize, then the Class 6 boulder-smashing falls, and then the very dangerous falls at the second railroad bridge, each separated by continuous, technically difficult water.

SHUTTLE: The shuttle for this trip is very long, but we recommend driving from the take-out at Bemis back to Glady. Continue on through Glady, turning right just beyond the town on FS 44. It is 25 miles through Wildell and May to Durbin. Turn right on US 250 and on up the mountain to FS 92 (third right). Follow the signs to McGee Run, the end of the Fish-for-Fun section of Shavers Fork. These roads are not plowed during the snow season.

GAUGE: Use the CR 33/8 gauge described below (section E). A 1- to 2-foot reading will be necessary, and at 2 feet those miles below High Falls will be very interesting. The Parsons gauge can be used as a rule of thumb by subtracting 2.5 and halving the remainder.

D. Bemis to the Bowden Bridge—9 Miles
(to CR 33/8 Bridge—14 Miles)

CLASS	GRADIENT	VOLUME	SCENERY	TIME	LEVEL
	3@65				
2–4	6@30	544	A–B	2	1–1.5′

MAPS: USGS—Glady and Bowden
        Monongahela National Forest
        COUNTY—Randolph

DESCRIPTION: What a way to start a canoe trip! The first 3 miles are straight downhill at a Class 4 pace, the next 3 are a delightful Class 3, while the last section levels out and divides into many small channels that provide a rather boring anticlimax. The river tumbles down vigorously off Cheat Mountain over beds of large boulders and provides very beautiful scenery (for the hiker; paddlers are so occupied, they don't see any scenery).

DIFFICULTIES: This section of the Cheat should be attempted only by advanced paddlers. If you have to get out and scout any of it, you are probably not ready for it. A smashup leaves one stranded in the wilderness, although one can walk out on the railroad right-of-way. After completing about a mile and a half of Class 3–4 rapids, you enter a very long (almost ¾ mile) rapids that is more complex than mean. There are plenty of small eddies behind boulders, so you can "stairstep" your way down gradually. After this very long rapids, there is a quiet pool, followed by a 50-yard lulu that contains 3 healthy souse holes which are best avoided. This is easier said than done, however, as the heavy current tends to send the boat in their direction. The river tames down considerably after this, but the paddler still needs to pay attention. There is 1 tricky place in the second section which seemingly is blocked by huge boulders, and finding a passage may be difficult. There is a dam immediately under the Bowden bridge. Below this dam is a 5-mile stretch of water that follows the highway until the CR 33/8 bridge is reached. This section contains just a few riffles and is rather boring due to the presence of many fishing cabins, trailer camps, and the like. Along this section one should visit the Bowden National Fish Hatchery.

SHUTTLE: Take out just upstream of Bowden bridge. The bridge can be seen from US 33. Bemis is reached by turning south from Alpena and taking "27" up to Glady. Turn right in Glady and take the 2-mile road into Bemis. Put in under the bridge.

GAUGE: See section E, below.

E. CR 33/8 Bridge to Parsons—22 Miles

CLASS	GRADIENT	VOLUME	SCENERY	TIME	LEVEL
1–2	19	544	A–B	6–7	1–2.5'

MAPS: USGS—Elkins, Bowden, and Parsons
Monongahela National Forest
COUNTIES—Randolph and Tucker

DESCRIPTION: This part of the Cheat is a pleasant interlude between its raucous birthplace high on Bald Knob and the pastoral serenity of the Cheat Valley from Parsons to Rowlesburg where the mighty river begins its furious cascade through Cheat Canyon. The water volume in this section is fairly large, but soon doubles when it joins the Black Fork in Parsons. This river, one of the state's most scenic, will appeal to the novice as well as to the expert. There are many ideal camping places and several vigorous rapids for playing around. The action and current are almost continuous with very little quiet water. The scenery through the deep hollows is spectacular. Many rocky bluffs and waterfalls line the river, while the shores are studded with magnificent growths of hemlock. Some of the rapids reach a Class 3 rating at the higher water levels, but the novice can always find an easier passage if he desires.

SHUTTLE: Can be set up in smaller segments. CR 33/8 to the steel bridge near Clifton Run is 6 miles by car, 8 by boat. From here on, the road on the right side of the river is rough. It comes close to the river at several points. If you want to do the whole thing, drive into Elkins and take US 219 to Parsons.

GAUGE: Located on the west bridge support on the upstream side of the CR 33/8 put-in. Subtract 2.5 from the Parsons government gauge on the Cheat and halve the remainder for an approximation.

To try to avoid confusion on the location of this bridge and gauge, this is the old US 33 bridge now bypassed by the new US 33 higher on the mountain. It is the bridge near the Stuart Recreation Area. CR 33/8, which may also be marked only as CR 33, can be accessed at Bowden if you are traveling west or at the top of the mountain when leaving Elkins if you are traveling east.

CHEAT RIVER

A. Parsons to Rowlesburg—36 Miles

CLASS	GRADIENT	VOLUME	SCENERY	TIME	LEVEL
B-1	7	1,653	B	10	3–4.5'

MAPS: USGS—Parsons, Saint George, and Rowlesburg
Monongahela National Forest
COUNTIES—Tucker and Preston

DESCRIPTION: This is a lazy but extremely beautiful river meandering alternately through well-kept farmland and spectacular bluffs. There are occasional Class 1 rapids that offer no problems unless the water is very high. One of the better rapids is just before the Holly Meadows bridge (3 miles from Parsons). The next bridge, 8 miles downstream, leads to the historic village of Saint George. About 2 miles below Saint George the river leaves the highway and enters a beautiful gorge. Some nice rapids occur here also.

Below Hannahsville the area known as Seven Islands is encountered and is particularly scenic. The highway does not come near this section, but there is a dirt road along the left side of the river. There are many deep pools suitable for swimming and fishing. Bass may be taken all along the river, while trout may be caught in the riffles of the upper stretches. Many primitive camping sites exist, and the river is ideal for extended open-boat touring.

It is recommended that all paddlers tour this scenic river and join in the fight against the Corps of Engineers and its plan to build a reservoir here.

SHUTTLE: Due to the nearness of roads, a shuttle can be set up most anywhere for shorter runs, particularly along WV 72.

GAUGE: See section D, below.

B. Rowlesburg to Albright Power Dam—14 Miles

CLASS	GRADIENT	VOLUME	SCENERY	TIME	LEVEL
2–4	5@20	2,207	C	3–4	0–4'

MAPS: USGS—Rowlesburg and Kingwood 7½'
         COUNTY—Preston

DESCRIPTION: Leaving Rowlesburg quietly and broadly, the river soon becomes narrower and starts to pick up speed. Approximately 3 miles below Rowlesburg, after having passed several Class 1–2 riffles, you encounter the first big waves, which are opposite a worked-out limestone mine (Cave Rapids). For the next 5 miles the rapids become increasingly more difficult. There are good rescue spots after each rapids, but in high water (3–4 feet) it's not so easy. After passing several Class 3 rapids, the paddler enters a long series of similar rapids, the "Narrows." The entire river is necked down by the presence of an automobile-sized boulder (Calamity Rock) in midstream which makes passage at any level difficult. Although this boulder is largely out of the water at 1 foot on the Albright gauge, it is completely submerged when the reading is a little over 2 feet. This should give the paddler a healthy respect for what just a few inches increase in water level means on the Cheat. Usually one should run the boulder on the passage to the right. At very high levels, however, it's best to run along the left bank, whether in boat or afoot. Keep in mind that there are 2 problems— entering the passage correctly, which is not always easy due to the combination of waves immediately above it, and managing the powerful drop at the end of the chute. This passage will swamp an open canoe at any level and will flip a raft in high water.

There are 3 major rapids below this boulder that also pass through narrow confines. This creates a tremendous turbulence and results in powerful crosscurrents and eddies. In high water one simply blasts through the standing 5-foot waves and tries to maintain stability, while at lower levels one must be more precise in maneuvering around the exposed boulders. The paddler inexperienced with big water might be fooled into thinking that he can "sneak" down the sides of these narrow rapids in the relatively calmer water, but usually he gets sucked over into the big stuff by the high velocity of the main channel (sort of like Bernoulli's principle).

The first of these major rapids (Wind Rapids) is the most difficult in high water and consists of a wide hydraulic before one reaches the chute. The hydraulic is best taken on the far left. There is also a severe hydraulic about halfway down the chute on the left, always an interesting scene. The second rapids (Rocking Horse) is the longest narrow

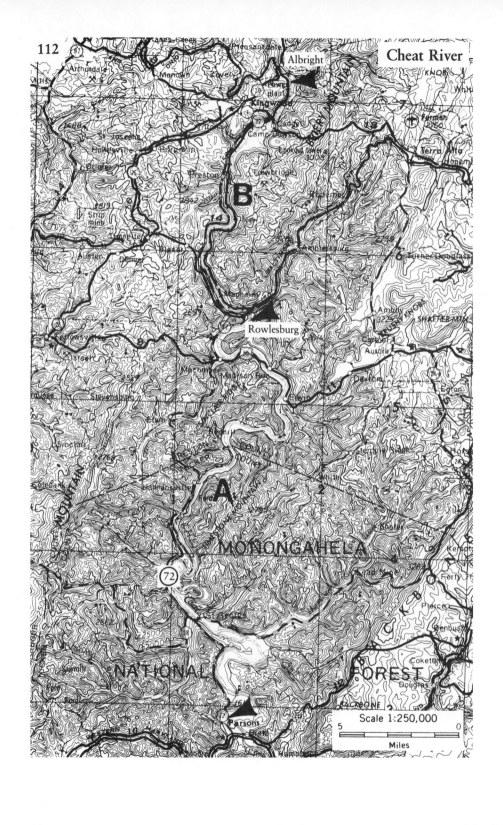

Scale 1:250,000

Miles

passage, 100 yards of turbulence. The last rapids is less severe but still interesting. In the remaining rapids to the railroad bridge, the paddler must concentrate on dodging boulders and catching the best chutes. By now, strip mine pollution has seriously damaged and scarred the river. The scenery at Preston is depressing, and the river again widens out leaving few places for rapids to form. Two miles below the WV 7 bridge there is a short Class 2 rapids, but nothing except the scenery improves very much. WV 72 parallels the river on the left as far as the bridge, while a local road continues on the right below it giving plenty of opportunity for scouting and/or setting up shorter trips.

SHUTTLE: Rowlesburg City park is a good put-in, while the right side of the river 200–300 yards above the Albright Power Station provides a take-out. Paddlers interested in the choicest part may put in opposite the limestone caves and take out at the mouth of Lick Run for a 5-mile trip.

GAUGE: See section D, below.

C. Albright WV 26 Bridge to Jenkinsburg Bridge—11 Miles

CLASS	GRADIENT	VOLUME	SCENERY	TIME	LEVEL
3–4	25	2,207	A	4	-0.5–7'

MAPS: USGS—Kingwood and Valley Point
COUNTY—Preston

DESCRIPTION: This beautiful wilderness river was once regarded as one of the most difficult rivers in the East. Since then, the Cheat Canyon has been moved down a few notches as better paddling skills have evolved and new rivers like the Gauley have been "discovered." However, this does not mean that the river has gotten any easier and it should not be taken lightly, especially by those unskilled at intricate maneuvering and in handling heavy water. At low water it is a notorious boat buster, and at high levels it has been a killer, literally. Massive boulders litter the riverbed, blocking the view through each rapids and contributing to the complexity of the run.

Some chutes of the canyon are very narrow, but the river gauge at the Albright bridge is located in a wide shallow spot. Hence, a 2-inch difference on the gauge makes a whale of a difference downstream, translating into feet in many instances. Anyone undertaking this run

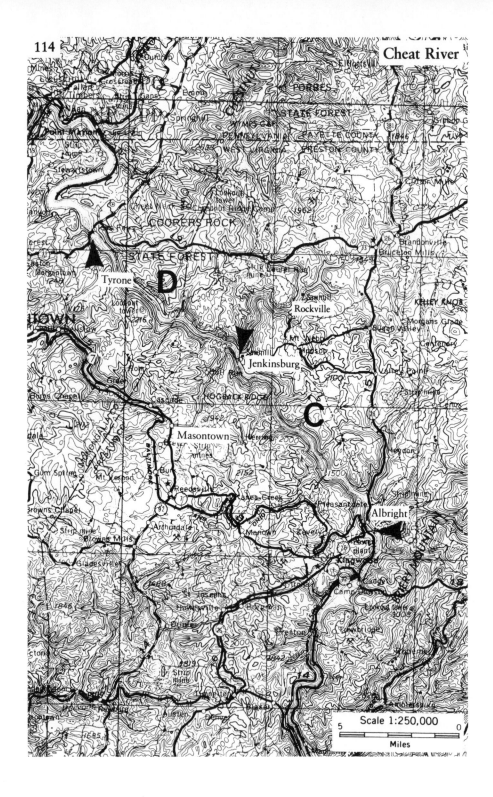

Cheat River

Scale 1:250,000

Miles

should realize that this is a very long run far from any roads. A smash-up puts the paddler miles from any help in country that is extremely difficult to traverse by foot. To walk out of the canyon straight up takes 2 hours and you still may be miles from the nearest farmhouse. There is a good trail on the right side of the river, but it is much higher than the river.

A detailed description of all of the difficult rapids in the Cheat Canyon is impractical due to their number and complexity (there are at least 38 of Class 3 or greater difficulty). There are no long flat pools, although each set of rapids is separated from the next by a small quiet spot.

DIFFICULTIES: The first rapids is a long, wide rock garden which soon narrows down and drops over a series of eroded ledges. There are some major hydraulics here in a complex countercurrent. If this is too much, take out immediately on the right because this will be your last chance to do so and they don't get any easier. If you count this as no. 1, the ninth major rapids should be approached with caution. Called Old Nasty, it is a 50-yard, furious drop over a boulder garden. You can't see the bottom from the top of the rapids, but enter at left center and gradually work to the right, carefully avoiding unpadded boulders. You should end up somewhat right of center.

Two rapids below this the paddler will encounter Even Nastier, a very long rapids. About two-thirds down, the main stream drops over a ledge on the left, through a hydraulic, then smacks into an enormous boulder, and peels off into a whirling hole on the left side. Since it's a long swim from here to the next pool, it is best to run this rapids on the tight left or to the right of the Even Nastier boulder.

About two-thirds of the way through the run, a louder than usual roar comes from a spectacularly beautiful right-hand turn along a sheer cliff. High Falls Rapids, named either for the 60-foot falls entering the river from the cliff or because it was once a high falls itself, consists of a shallow, wide reef dropping steeply into a natural amphitheater. Finding the correct passage over the reef can only be done by scouting or following someone familiar with the route. A good passage at most levels is over the highest center green wave visible on approach and then being swept to the left by the current.

The next rapids gets harder at lower water. In this Maze Rapids the paddler often gets sucked into a dead end. The second rapids below High Falls, known as the Trap, is very long, steep, and complicated.

Trap Rapids demands a great deal of maneuvering from the right side of the river to the left and then back again through heavy drops. In high water it is a real brawler. Don't miss the beautiful right-side waterfall high along this rapids. Try to miss Box Canyon, Devil's Trap, and Pillow Rock. The next rapids, named in honor of Pete Morgan of Albright who for many years was a helpful friend to all Cheat paddlers, begins at the far left. A huge white boulder, Picture Rock, may be seen at the far right. Paddle toward it and eddy out behind it. Straight downstream is a steep descent into a complex current, which curiously enough gets harder at lower water levels. At low water it is a double diagonal hydraulic and the problem is to stay aligned between the two. In the pool below, the paddler should pause to marvel at the fluted columns carved into the base of the Greenbrier limestone. This gives the rapids its other name, Coliseum.

There are more goodies, but they begin to ease up until a flat pool is reached beneath the Jenkinsburg bridge. One more warning—this river can go up very fast. It has been known to rise 2 feet while a run was in progress!

SHUTTLE: Put in at the Albright bridge or, to avoid some flat, uninteresting water, at a campground about a mile downstream on WV 26. There is a fee for using the latter. The take-out at Jenkinsburg is not easy to find. Take WV 26 south to Kingwood and go right on WV 7 to Masontown. Turn right at the drugstore on Main and Depot streets and take this road to the fork. Turn left and continue on to Bull Run and a second fork. Take this to the right down the extremely steep, narrow road to Jenkinsburg. A shorter but rougher shuttle is via Valley Point and Mount Nebo on the right side of the river. (See Big Sandy shuttle and map on page 126.) From the river, paddle on down below the bridge to the mouth of the Big Sandy. An easy trail leads up to the parking area.

GAUGE: See section D, below.

D. Jenkinsburg Bridge to Cheat Lake—8 Miles

CLASS	GRADIENT	VOLUME	SCENERY	TIME	LEVEL
3,B,A	4@16	2,632	A	3	0–4'

MAPS: USGS—Masontown and Lake Lynn
COUNTIES—Preston and Monongalia

DESCRIPTION: This interesting run is seldom paddled because there are only 4 miles of rapids followed by a long flat paddle and the shuttle takes so long. It is a good indication of what some of the easier rapids in the upper canyon are like. The first rapids is encountered about 50 yards below the mouth of the Big Sandy, with the best passage toward the right in low water. If this is too low, forget it. One will encounter 4 good rapids (Class 3) and several riffles in the first 4 miles. The last rapids is divided by a gravel bar (Grassy Island). High above this island on the right is the impressive Coopers Rock State Park. In our experience, the only dangers on the trip have been the risk of being run over by powerboat cowboys and, on at least one occasion, a damned seaplane! The long flat paddle to the take-out is beautiful but very wearisome kneeling in a C-1. Soon Mont Chateau State Park is reached, but there is no easy take-out there. You'll have to pay to take out at the marina next door, so you may as well paddle on down to the "857" bridge.

SHUTTLE: Horrendous! Jenkinsburg is described above in section C. To reach the take-out, go back out to Masontown, turn right on WV 7, and head for Dellslow or Pioneer Rocks. Turn right on Tyrone Road, "75," and go to "857". Turn right and drive to the east side of the bridge.

GAUGE: The 3 lower parts of the Cheat (sections B, C, and D) can be run year around, even often during the summer, but one must be careful that the river is not too high. It is a huge watershed and the river is very powerful in high water. The canoeing gauge is located on the Albright bridge, and the reading may be obtained by calling Morgan's Gas Station at 329-1748. The Parsons gauge reading may be obtained by calling the National Weather Service in Pittsburgh at (412) 644-2890. There you will get a Parsons gauge and an Albright bridge reading. If only one is given, then a conversion between the two gauges may be obtained: Parsons gauge $-2.3 = \frac{3}{4}$ Albright gauge. It is a good run at 1 to 4 feet.

HORSESHOE RUN

Shafer to Bridge Above Saint George—9 Miles

CLASS	GRADIENT	VOLUME	SCENERY	TIME	LEVEL
1–3	41	S	B	3	6'

MAPS: USGS—Saint George and Lead Mine
COUNTY:—Tucker

DESCRIPTION: This is a simple, clear little stream draining the northernmost portion of the Monongahela National Forest and flowing past Forest Service and YMCA camps bearing the same name. The run is named for the huge loop in the Cheat just upstream from the mouth of this run. If the Rowlesburg Dam goes in, the lower 3 miles of this beautiful stream will be ruined.

After 2.6 miles of uncomplicated moving water, the paddler negotiates a series of low ledges near Lead Mine. One mile downstream, the river passes under the bridge going up Hile Run. Between here and the YMCA camp is the most interesting section with the run channeling and dropping over easy Class 3 ledges. From Camp Horseshoe to the bridge near the mouth are easy gravel bars with half the gradient of the upper stream.

DIFFICULTIES: There are essentially no difficulties except catching this tiny trout stream when it is high enough to run. While it is an easy run suitable for the novice, it is not a bore to the intermediate or advanced paddler because of the continuous drop and scenic surroundings. Caution: If you happen to catch it up in the summer, each of the camps may not have had time to take down temporary dams made out of pipes and planks. These could be dangerous.

SHUTTLE: Put-in can be reached from WV 72 by driving through Saint George and out "1" to Camp Horseshoe, on to Lead Mine, and then on "7" to Shafer where several small streams join to form Horseshoe Run. The first bridge you cross on your way from Saint George is the take-out.

GAUGE: None. The level refers to the Parsons gauge and is only a general guide. The bridge on the side road up Hile Run should not be showing more than 7 stones on the right-side abutment to have adequate volume.

BUFFALO CREEK

WV 72 to Macomber—4.5 Miles

CLASS	GRADIENT	VOLUME	SCENERY	TIME	LEVEL
3	86	S	A	1	1.6–2.2'

MAPS: USGS—Rowlesburg
      COUNTY—Preston

DESCRIPTION: A ride on Buffalo Creek is better than any mechanical bull. It's very steep, very narrow, and very enjoyable. The only difficulty occurs just below the second bridge, where a blind bend hides 3 medium-sized ledges. You might wish to scout here.

SHUTTLE: Put in a mile below Etam at a bridge. Shuttle on WV 72. Take out at US 50 bridge.

GAUGE: There is a gauge on the left below the second bridge encountered.

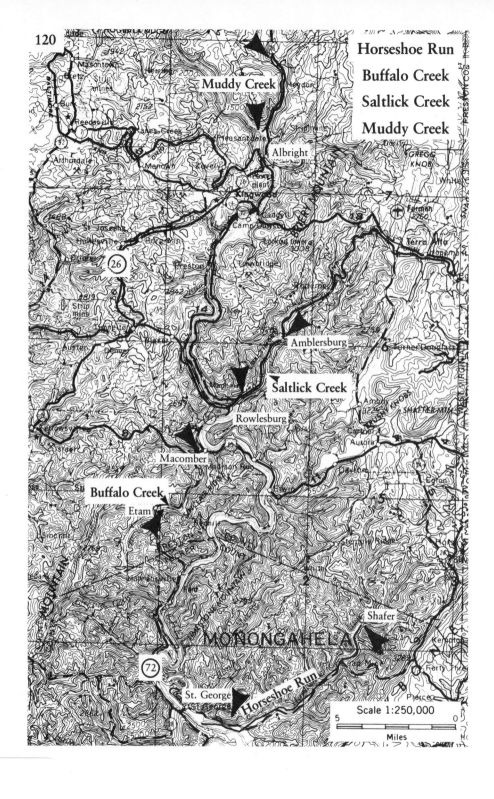

Horseshoe Run
Buffalo Creek
Saltlick Creek
Muddy Creek

Scale 1:250,000
Miles

SALTLICK CREEK

Amblersburg to Rowlesburg—4 Miles

CLASS	GRADIENT	VOLUME	SCENERY	TIME	LEVEL
3	52	S	B	1	–

MAPS: USGS—Kingwood and Rowlesburg
COUNTY—Preston

DESCRIPTION: This is the thing to do when the Cheat is too high and it has been raining steadily for a day. The run is parallel to the main line of the B&O as it descends Briery Mountain from Terra Alta.

At adequate water levels the water is continuous Class 3 with some stoppers and haystacks. There is a 5-foot dam at the B&O switching yards that can be run but is usually carried.

DIFFICULTIES: Higher on this little tributary, logs and trees are a significant hazard, and in this section they are still a potential threat. Look out for the dam.

SHUTTLE: CR 51 parallels the full length of the creek.

GAUGE: None. When Calamity Rock on the Cheat Narrows cannot be located, and the Parsons gauge is 6 feet, and there isn't time to get to the upstream tribs of the Cheat, go for it.

MUDDY CREEK

WV 26 Bridge to Cheat River—2.5 Miles

CLASS	GRADIENT	VOLUME	SCENERY	TIME	LEVEL
4	92	S	B	1	0–1′

MAPS: USGS—Valley Point
     COUNTY—Preston

DESCRIPTION: It's dodge 'em all the way—rocks and logging debris, that is. The creek runs entirely along WV 26. Stop and visit the antique iron furnace midway along this roller coaster for a view of the Big Muddy Rift. Below the rift the run is a series of boulders.

DIFFICULTIES: Below the put-in is Little Muddy Rift, a narrow, twisting drop of 10 feet in 20 feet with undercut rocks. A mile later the river drops over Big Muddy Rift, a wide, slanting shelf about 20 feet high and 100 yards long. This is a very steep young stream with few eddies and sharp rocks. Because of upstream logging there is a danger of being forced into a jam of debris.

SHUTTLE: Put in at WV 26 bridge. Take out at the side road bridge in sight of the Cheat.

GAUGE: The above readings are for the Little Sandy. This is the next watershed north along WV 26 and would reflect the same necessarily wet conditions.

BIG SANDY CREEK OF PRESTON COUNTY

The Big Sandy Creek of Preston County from the Pennsylvania-West Virginia state line to Bruceton Mills is a 5-mile run with no danger spots. This is a very small, intimate stream with a 3 fpm gradient flowing through rhododendron thickets and small farms. The bed is sandy to muddy, but there is good fishing for trout and bass. The best rapids are at Clifton Mills. All flat water from here to the dam. Put in at the steel bridge on the road north of Brandonville, West Virginia. The put-in is actually on a tributary of the Big Sandy, Little Sandy Creek. (This should not be confused with another Little Sandy Creek, page 127.) The take-out is on the right above the dam at Bruceton Mills. Be careful in high water.

A. Bruceton Mills to Rockville—6 Miles

CLASS	GRADIENT	VOLUME	SCENERY	TIME	LEVEL
	4@9				
1–4	2@45	415	A	2	5.8–7'

MAPS: USGS—Valley Point and Bruceton Mills
 COUNTY—Preston

DESCRIPTION: This is 6 miles of progressive slalom training starting at Class 1 and sequentially working up to Class 4 as this little stream tips down beside Chestnut Ridge to the Cheat Gorge. Suitable for intermediate paddlers in open boats at lower water levels, but decking is recommended. Automobile camping is provided at nearby Cooper's Rock State Park.

DIFFICULTIES: Hazel Run Rapids is the first problem and appears as an impassable barricade of boulders. Try the second passage from the right. Below the mouth of the Little Sandy (on the left), one will encounter a long slide rapids where the water zips quickly over very shallow rock tables and then terminates in several wide hydraulics. Below the mouth about 500 yards is a 6-to 8-foot falls. It can be recognized easily by the large shelf of rock jutting out from the left forming a dam. The first shelf can be carefully run by cutting hard left below this ledge then back across to near center for the main ledge. At higher levels run straight over left or far right.

A very long rapids or one rapids right after the other occurs just below the falls, and this is where the big action is found. Several steep drops over ledges around blind bends require quick decisions and paddle responses. This continues until the take-out. It is usually a good Class 4 except in very low water. Paddlers in trouble may want to take out at the rustic cabin on the right just below the mouth of Laurel Run and Corner Rapids. The approach to the bridge is tricky. At normal water levels, it's easiest to start in the center and then cut sharply to the right. At high levels the far left is no problem.

SHUTTLE: Put in below the dam at Bruceton Mills. Take out just under the Rockville bridge on the left. When parking, be careful not to block access to the cottages. Rockville can be reached from "73/73" crossing over Laurel Run. Take the left fork twice. The Big Sandy can also be run starting on Laurel Run at "73/73."

GAUGE: See section B, below.

B. Rockville to Cheat River—5.5 Miles

CLASS	GRADIENT	VOLUME	SCENERY	TIME	LEVEL
	2@30				
4–5	4@80	415	A	3	5.8–6.5'

MAPS: USGS—Bruceton Mills and Valley Point
        COUNTY—Preston

DESCRIPTION: The lower Big Sandy is an exciting, beautiful, piquant mistress who shows occasional flares of bad temper to even the most experienced canoeists. This is the most remote, most scenic, and most challenging whitewater in northern West Virginia. The banks are choked with laurel, making the necessary scouting and portaging very difficult. If a walk-out is necessary there is an old railroad bed on the right to within a mile of the Cheat River. Then you would have to figure out how to get over to the left where the only road reaches the river at Jenkinsburg.

DIFFICULTIES: Plenty! Parts of the course are hazardous and require scouting and carrying. At 1.5 miles there is a rather difficult sequence terminating in 18-foot falls. It begins with a fairly steep 3-part drop on the left into a pool just above the falls. Scout and use safety measures. Carry the falls on the right. The falls can be run on the left side of the main current. The next series of rapids is busy for a quarter mile, followed by a broad ledge split by a large rock in midstream. The passage on the right ends in a big curler which throws good boaters under an undercut rock. Run more safely just to the left of center. The next biggie is Zoom Flume, a steep 8- to 10-foot drop which is easier than it looks and even more exciting. Scouting is again recommended to see the twisting flume. The cheese-grater rock shelf below has taken off a lot of elbow skin. Get back out of your boat if you are still in it and scout the next rapids, Little Splat. It is safest to finish on the right. The second falls, Big Splat, is next and is a complex falls dropping a total of 25 feet. Clearly a Class 6 rapids. Carry on the right. In the section below here, there are 2 islands. Run both on the right. Three and a half miles and 272 feet (down) later, the paddler, who may be hiking by now, will reach the Cheat River near Jenkinsburg.

SHUTTLE: Put in at Rockville (see section A, above). The take-out is on the left at the mouth of Big Sandy on the Cheat. Take the steep trail up through the laurel thicket to the parking area. Jenkinsburg may be reached by continuing on the road from Rockville (from the left side of the river)—turn right at the top of the hill, then take a left at the next crossing and proceed to Mount Nebo School. At Mount Nebo bear hard right to Jenkinsburg. This is terrible driving and almost as rough as the paddling.

GAUGES: The reading above refers to a government gauge on the bridge at Rockville. There is a paddler's gauge under the Bruceton Mills bridge. The correlation between the two is complex but good. Rockville $= \frac{3}{4}$ (Bruceton $+ 1$) $+ 5$. The recommended levels at Bruceton are 0–2 feet. The painted gauge is awfully hard to read now.

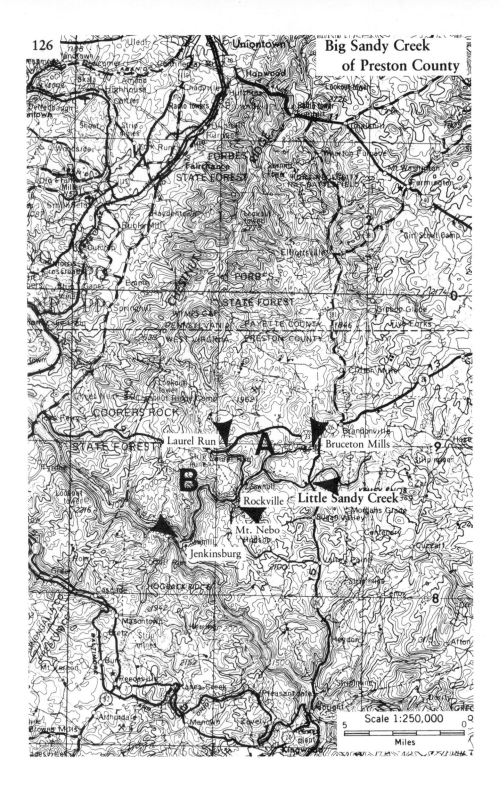

Big Sandy Creek
of Preston County

Scale 1:250,000

Miles

LITTLE SANDY CREEK

Little Sandy to Rockville—5 Miles

CLASS	GRADIENT	VOLUME	SCENERY	TIME	LEVEL
3–4	41(1@70)	S	A	2	6.5–7.5'

MAPS: USGS—Bruceton Mills
       COUNTY—Preston

DESCRIPTION: A tougher whitewater trip than the Bruceton to Rockville section, requiring a more skilled paddler and more water. It is wilderness all the way. After a 20-minute paddle on flat water, the first of several ledges is reached. The river then becomes a very continuous Class 3 rapids dropping 70 feet in 1 mile. The last 2 miles of this trip are on the tough part of a swollen Big Sandy. Note that the level required to get down the Little Sandy puts the Big Sandy above the recommended level for its section A where the Little Sandy enters (see p. 123). If you are feeling confident, the run from WV 26 to Jenkinsburg, section B of the Big Sandy, will be one of the most memorable whitewater trips of a lifetime.

DIFFICULTIES: Finding the smoothest passage over some of the smaller ledges is sometimes difficult, but remember, it's only a boat. A sloping ledge on the Little Sandy is complicated by a boulder standing at the bottom catching the main current. Take care to avoid a pinning at lower levels. Avoid it to the left at higher levels. Also, all of the Big Sandy at this level is an interesting place.

SHUTTLE: Put in at WV 26 bridge 2 miles south of Bruceton Mills. The shuttle to Rockville is rough but direct. Take "26/16," right at fork on "14/3," then right again on "14" to bridge over Big Sandy.

GAUGE: The reading above refers to the Rockville gauge. There is a strange paddler's gauge at the put-in. It rarely reaches zero.

Middle Fork of the Tygart River

Photograph by Ward Eister.

3 Fastest Water to the North—The Tygart Sub-Basin

Of the rivers that flow out of the mountainous heartland north toward the Ohio, the Tygart ranks among the mightiest in the state. The Tygart begins high in the mountains of Randolph County, not too far from the headwaters of the Elk, and flows through a valley rich in history and natural beauty. Up there the river is known locally as "Tygart's Valley." Near Philippi, it picks up 2 very significant tributaries, the Middle Fork and the Buckhannon. It meets its sister river, the West Fork, in Fairmont to form the Monongahela.

The West Fork is fairly flat and winds gently through largely settled areas, whereas the Middle Fork, most of the Buckhannon, and part of the Tygart pass through extremely wild country. A minor but interesting tributary of the Tygart, Three Fork Creek, has its mouth in Grafton below the Tygart Reservoir, and the nearby trout stream, Whiteday Creek, has its mouth in the Monongahela not many miles away.

Much of the watershed receives acid pollution and siltation. The fact that there are no municipalities with secondary sewage treatment facilities, coupled with the industrial wastes of the lower valley, causes serious pollution on the lower watershed. The upper part of all the Tygart branches and tributaries are good trout streams and, near Huttonsville, offer superb bass fishing as well. The Buckhannon has suffered many devastating fish kills recently from abandoned mines. Strip mining on the Buckhannon and lower Tygart is routine.

State parks exist at Audra on the Middle Fork and at the spectacular Valley Falls on the lower Tygart. The Corps of Engineers has a dam above Grafton creating a reservoir, and there is a state park there as well. This reservoir has a phantasmagoric drawdown and is managed solely for navigation releases on the Monongahela, not at the barge companies' expense, but at yours. A new reservoir, Stonewall Jackson, is planned for the West Fork near Weston. This dam will create recognized benefits for the state in the way of flood control between Weston and Clarksburg and well-planned recreational facilities in conjunction with state agencies; it's also locally desired, thus making it somewhat unique in the state.

Points of interest on the Tygart include the area around Valley Head and Mingo Flats, long known as a site of Indian travel and encampment; Civil War trenches, and the site of Robert E. Lee's headquarters at one time near Huttonsville; and the site of the first land battle of the Civil War and the unusual double-lane covered bridge, both at Philippi. Ghost towns are common along the Buckhannon where mills once stood harnessing its power. Beverly, located on the Tygart above Elkins, was once the largest town around and the seat of Randolph County. Now Elkins is the county seat, and bitter animosities still remain between Beverly and Elkins because of this. Hammond, below Valley Falls, is also an interesting place, once the site of the largest brickyards in the East. At one time it was a very large community with trainloads of bricks leaving everyday. A disastrous fire, followed by some hanky-panky in the till, folded the industry in the early forties. The remains of the kilns exist today and are very interesting. The distinctive bricks made by the firm may be found everywhere in the vicinity.

The Tygart Valley in Randolph County has some nice farms in the rich bottoms and mines in the nearby mountains, but the main industry is timber and wood products, with Elkins as the center. Elkins is the host of the Mountain State Forest Festival held each year in early October and is also the headquarters of the Monongahela National Forest. It would be an ideal place for a whitewater paddler to live due to its proximity to so many superb rivers.

Barbour and Upshur counties do not have such supportive industries. The county seats of Philippi and Buckhannon are principally small college towns. Although these counties are not usually thought of as mountain counties, both are extremely rugged and underlain with vast coal deposits. Together with a poor alternative economic base, this factor has made them prime targets for the strippers' bulldozers. Taylor and Marion counties are small but underlain with rich natural gas fields. This and glassmaking are the supportive industries. Grafton was once an important railroad center, then declined, but is now returning economically. Fairmont is both a small college town and a busy industrial city.

TYGART RIVER

The Tygart Above Elkins — 32 + Miles

MAPS: USGS—Valley Head, Adolph, Mill Creek, Beverly West,
Beverly East, and Elkins
Monongahela National Forest
COUNTY—Randolph

From Mill Creek to the bridge at the western edge of Elkins is a distance of 32 miles. The river drops only 100 feet in this distance and rarely exceeds a Class 1 rating. It is a small river most of the way, getting larger near Elkins. The Tygart Valley is a broad, picturesque valley studded with prosperous farms and walled off in the distance by the mountains. The river meanders lazily through this scenic country but would only be canoeable during the spring or wet periods. The river has been run from as high as Valley Head, and some Class 2 is found between there and Huttonsville. Watch for fences and a 2-foot weir. We were impressed by the changing scenery and the tremendous amount of wildlife seen on the river. This part of the Tygart could be broken up into several such short runs.

A. Norton to Beaver Creek (the Tygart Loop)—5 Miles

CLASS	GRADIENT	VOLUME	SCENERY	TIME	LEVEL
3-5	25	790	C–D	2	4–5'

MAPS: USGS—Junior
Monongahela National Forest
COUNTIES—Randolph and Barbour

DESCRIPTION: The river from Elkins to Norton is rather slow and dreary, containing only a 3-foot ledge and a few riffles. At Harding the river leaves the highway and, like a naughty child, while it is hidden from sight it acts up, only to resume its party manners when it comes back to the road south of Junior. In general this is true with much of the Tygart. Where it can easily be seen, it looks like a Sunday float trip; where it cannot, it Class 5's you. Below Harding the river drops through long, challenging Class 3 rapids. It picks up as it tumbles over a rocky, eroded ledge veering to the right and ends squirting

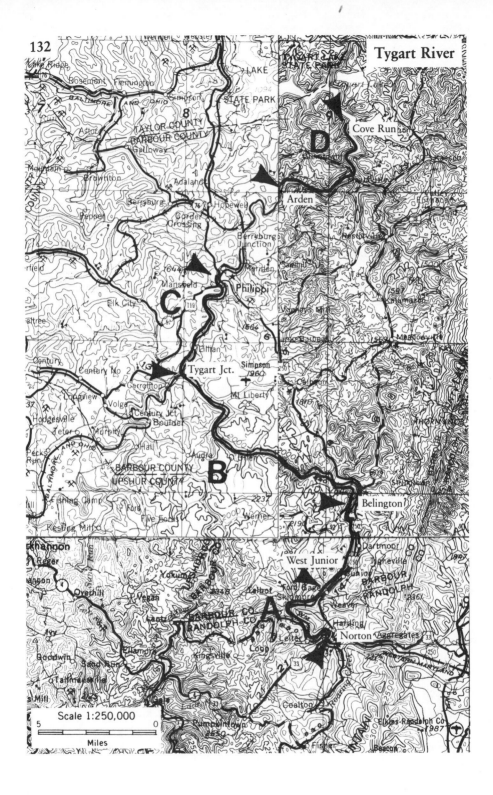

Scale 1:250,000

Miles

between 20-foot boulders in 3 channels, 10 feet each, which may be choked by obstructing logs. This Class 4 complex pauses in a small pool where the river turns sharply to the left, dropping 10 feet over a 50-yard sloping rock bed and disappearing around the next bend to the right behind the Twin Giants. Beyond this nightmare are 2 rapids with stoppers.

DIFFICULTIES: The Twin Giants are frightening. After the Class 4 rapids and pool described above, the 50-yard-long flow dropping out of the pool is punctuated by 3 diagonal stoppers, all slanting from left to right and driving the paddler toward a couple of 35-foot boulders which are perched on small pedestals. Most of the water gets around to the left of these huge rocks, but some runs out under them via a 30-foot-long tunnel, 4 feet high, 10 feet wide and 50–100% full of swirling water. It is no place to go, but the diagonal stoppers are shoving, shoving, shoving! This horror chamber is a likely place for a floating tree to lodge itself and become a very effective body snatcher. Scouting is a must and the carry on the right is tough.

SHUTTLE: Put in under the US 33 bridge at Norton reached from US 250 just north of its junction with US 33. Turn west and swing down around the hill to the left. The take-out is 3 miles north of US 250 south of Junior where the highway bridges Beaver Creek. The river from here into Belington is dull and unattractive.

GAUGE: In Belington a half mile downstream from bridge on left bank. Gauge can be read through the door or learned from the Pittsburgh Weather Service, (412) 644-2890.

B. Belington to the Mouth of the Buckhannon—11 Miles

CLASS	GRADIENT	VOLUME	SCENERY	TIME	LEVEL
3–5	37	790	A	3–4	2.5–6.8'

MAPS: USGS—Belington and Audra
       Monongahela National Forest
       COUNTY—Barbour

DESCRIPTION: This is the most rugged portion of the Tygart. The rapids are continuous, complex, and bodacious. The river tumbles through a spectacular gorge civilized only by the railroad tracks on the right bank. Incidentally, it is worth the slight disfigurement to have an emergency walkway to safety. The water, clean but acid-polluted, flows through second-growth deciduous and coniferous forests.

The trip starts out with a literal bang—3 huge ledges must first be negotiated. Then it is 1 narrow, steep rapids after another for several miles. In most of these rapids vision is limited by huge boulders. The river then broadens somewhat, and the rapids gentle down to a Class 2 or 3 level before joining the Middle Fork.

The current is then noticeably more forceful and, although the gradient hasn't picked up (yet), the rapids are heavier. In about 2 miles the paddler arrives at the most interesting part of the river. It necks down and drops 80 feet in about 1¼ miles, which is terrific for a river of such volume. After this there are many interesting rapids with absolutely sinister countercurrents, boils, and assorted goodies. Finally the river broadens out considerably and welcomes its sister, the Buckhannon.

DIFFICULTIES: About 3.7 miles below Belington or just below the alternative put-in, the river begins tumbling over 6- to 8-foot ledges between boxcar-sized boulders separated by 3- to 4-foot sluiceways. The first of these is Keyhole and consists of 2 very tiny passages that disappear between the huge boulders. In low water, you should take the one on your left (just a hair wider than your boat), making sure to hold your paddle in the vertical, rather than horizontal, position. You'll zoom down what looks like a gun barrel. (The right chute is better at high water.) The next 2 ledges are blind and ought to be scouted to find the correct passage. Some will want to carry the fourth one, Hard Tongue Falls, which roars over the ledge and caroms off a boulder wall on the left into an incredible cauldron of boiling foam. Below this, look for the Gates, a row of boulders across the river forming 3 slots. Run the middle drop please. The left is undercut.

In the steep section 2 miles below the mouth of the Middle Fork, the river pools against a riverwide barrage of boulders and then disappears to the left, dropping 25 feet through a Z-shaped chute 75 yards long. In general, run this the way most of the water does; start center, move left, then move right to avoid a left-side hole, and, finally finish left. (At high levels, you can sneak the Z by paddling down the right side to the bottom of the Z and dropping over a 5-foot ledge of boulders.) The very next rapids is a carry for many paddlers (on the right). This is Shoulder Snapper Falls, an 8-foot sheer drop into a pile of boulders. On one occasion when this falls was attempted, the boat got stuck in an almost vertical position behind boulders at the bottom. The unlucky paddler, who couldn't wiggle loose, dislocated his shoulder while attempting to leave his boat in the fast current. Another hit the rocks so hard he drove his foot brace into his shin and had to be hospitalized. On the other hand, plenty of water renders the right center a straight shot. In any event, scouting is advised. A half mile below Shoulder Snapper look for the Hook Drop. This is a sharp left turn in heavy water. Just below is Instant Ender. Save time for playing in this area.

SHUTTLE: Put in at the bridge in Belington or, to avoid 3 miles of uninteresting flat water, shuttle via Philippi, turning right off US 250 at Mt. Pleasant Road, then left for 0.7 mile, and right 1 mile down over something imitating a road to the riverbank (Papa Weese's Paradise, a fishing camp). Take-out is reached from US 119 taking "36" to Carrollton. Take the dirt road on the left side of the Buckhannon as far as you can or dare. This is privately owned. Please ask permission, close all gates, and park so as not to obstruct traffic. From the river, you must paddle upstream upon reaching the mouth of the Buckhannon and land on the sandy bank 100 yards upstream on your right. It's a tough take-out through a lot of brush. As of this writing, there are reports of this take-out being closed. This means paddling on to Philippi or, heaven forbid, carrying your boat up the railroad tracks to Carrollton. See shuttle for section C, below.

GAUGE: Pittsburgh National Weather Service office, (412) 644-2890. Ask for the Belington reading, which is located on the left bank in Belington and can be read directly.

C. Mouth of Buckhannon to Philippi—5.3 Miles

CLASS	GRADIENT	VOLUME	SCENERY	TIME	LEVEL
1-2	7	1,782	B–C	1.5	3–5'

MAPS: USGS—Audra and Philippi
       Monongahela National Forest
       COUNTY—Barbour

DESCRIPTION: This is a pleasant short trip close to Philippi consisting of several rapids curving gently around large boulders. At low-to medium-water levels (3.5–4.5 feet), the rapids are of Class 1–2 difficulty, but they could become more difficult in high water since all of the rapids are formed at narrow spots in the river. The scenery begins in a nice woodsy setting but soon breaks down when an extremely long strip mine is encountered on the left bank. This gives way to pastoral hillsides and then the small college town of Philippi. The first half of the trip contains most of the action while the latter is mostly flat. Contrary to what the Philippi topo map shows, there are no "falls" on this section and it is an excellent undecked boat run. There is 1 riverwide ledge (2 feet in low water) just above the historic, double-lane covered bridge and in sight of Alderson-Broaddus College which is high on the hill in the background. Run at center. Below the bridge is a 5.5-mile flat-water paddle through mostly depressing scenery until the first rapids of the Arden Run are encountered.

SHUTTLE: It is suggested that one put in at Carrollton on the Buckhannon River, which is only ¾ mile above the mouth for a total run of 6 miles. (Buckhannon River is a smaller stream of Class 1–3 rating at this point with fairly continuous action over easy drops and around corners.) The put-in at a covered bridge in Carrollton is reached by turning onto "36" from US 119 south of Philippi. This is a uniquely historic run in that rare covered bridges may be found both at the put-in and the take-out.

GAUGE: See Section D, below.

D. 2 Miles Above Arden to Big Cove Run—8 Miles

CLASS	GRADIENT	VOLUME	SCENERY	TIME	LEVEL
3–5	27	1,782	C	3	2.5–4.5'

MAPS: USGS—Philippi and Nestorville
       Monongahela National Forest (good for shuttle roads)
       COUNTY—Barbour

DESCRIPTION: The Tygart is a big flat river for 5.5 miles below Philippi while it gathers courage for the 170-foot jump to the reservoir behind the Grafton dam. All but the last 3 miles of the run below Arden may be scouted from a secondary road which runs from Philippi to the ancient concrete bridge at Teter Creek. Some of the best water is in the remaining run to the reservoir. The river drops over big rock ledges and reefs and is strewn with huge boulders. As one approaches the reservoir during the drawdown season, ugly mud slopes detract from the otherwise remoteness of the area.

DIFFICULTIES: About 1 mile below Arden there is a ledge channeled on the left. The current continues down the left side 50 feet, dropping over a boulder and ending in 2 stoppers. The larger upstream wave must be skirted to the right if one is to maintain alignment and speed for running a ledge and the second stopper. In the second rapids downstream from Laurel Creek (which enters from the right under a steel bridge), the river narrows and piles over a rapid succession of 3 ledges with unavoidable 5-foot standing waves. Three hundred yards below this rapids, the river funnels over a ledge to the left and undercuts a shelf of rock with a 1-foot clearance. This can be negotiated, but it is dangerous.

Five hundred yards farther downstream the river spills over a 15- to 20-foot riverwide falls. This can be scrambled on the right at low water after sneaking under the natural bridge. More recently paddlers have run this falls right over the middle—a 15-foot drop into soft suds. For the squeamish and/or less advanced boater, it may be better to carry along the road on the right. One mile below this the river is narrowed and split by a partially submerged, house-sized boulder in a powerful drop. It is fairly flat until the Teter Creek bridge.

About 2 miles below Teter Creek bridge is a game called Blindman's Bluff. The river pools up behind a natural rock dam, turns to the left and immediately to the right, all of the time being necked down considerably. There are big diagonal stoppers pushing to the right in this turn, and as you regain alignment around the last corner, you are faced with a huge tongue of water called Well's Falls dropping 10 feet over a slide into a formidable stopper. If you slide off the left-side tongue to the right, you will slam into a 4-foot wall of water. This is the most powerful, runnable rapids in the entire Monongahela Basin and should be scouted each time. The very next rapids is also mean—essentially a sheer drop into a very nasty hole. Both of these rapids are runnable, but they are also easily carried on the right. All of the other rapids below Teter Creek are nice Class 3 drops that offer no special problems (in low water). The entire Arden section is something to avoid during periods of high water. This can get awfully messy in the spring.

SHUTTLE: From Arden use the dirt road on the right side of the river for the shuttle. Drive about 2 miles upstream to the first rapids for an easy put-in. Beginners should take out at the Arden bridge. Intermediates can take out at Laurel Creek. Experts proceed with caution and scout the falls. One can take out at Teter Creek for an easy shuttle with a road alongside throughout. To reach the Cove Run take-out,

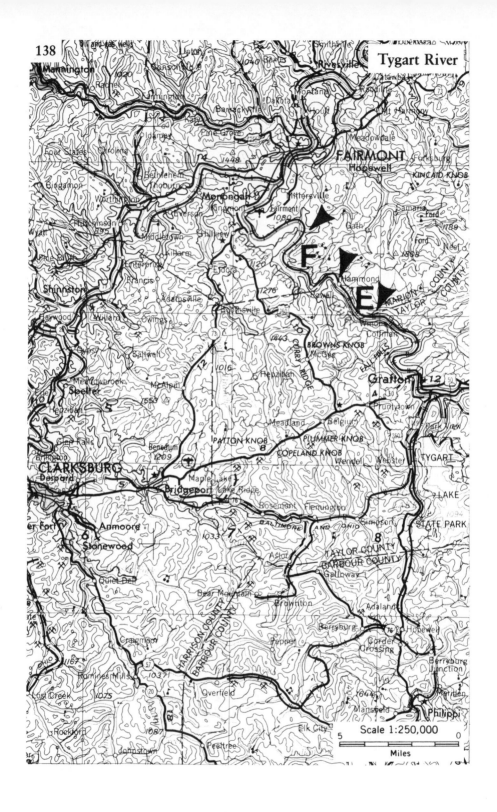

Tygart River

Scale 1:250,000

Miles

turn right at Teter Creek and go out to the main highway, WV 92, and turn left. Take Cove Run Road "2" to the left, then a right, another right, and then a left at the succeeding forks. The last part takes you down a very steep unimproved road to the river. Be sure you recognize this point from the river. You will not find rapids on the lower part until around the first of October. Peak drawdown is generally reached about the last of February. At such time there is another 1.8 miles of rapids dropping 30 fpm. You then have another 2 miles of flat water to take-out on the left side at Wildcat Hollow Boat Club.

GAUGE: One can call the Pittsburgh Weather Service, (412) 644-2890, and ask for the Tygart River reading at Philippi. These are the readings referred to above.

E. Valley Falls to Hammond—1.5 Miles

CLASS	GRADIENT	VOLUME	SCENERY	TIME	LEVEL
2–6	60	2,259	A	1	0–1'

MAPS: USGS—Fairmont East
         COUNTY—Marion

DESCRIPTION: This section of the Tygart should be considered an expedition requiring a close scrutiny of the dam discharge from Grafton and a certain cavalier attitude. The major difficulty in addition to the gradient is the fact that this section of the river has been narrowed down 80% as it enters the steep gorge. This is considerable for such a large volume of water. In this section there are several major drops. The first ledge, Valley Falls, is about 10 miles downstream from Grafton. It is the site of an old mill, artifacts of which still remain. This is a riverwide ledge about 7 feet high which has water coming over at at least 3 sites (low-water level). The chute on the right is sloping and can be run with more water, although it does pile angrily into and off the shore rocks at its base. The next ledge of about 14 feet is sharp and appears unrunnable. At low water it can be run to the left of the right half. At higher water the boat disappears deep into a pool and pops up into the falls where it stays and stays and stays. The third ledge is a Class 4 rapids with 2 runnable channels, both requiring right-angle turns to the left after running tight along the right bank. The fourth ledge is clearly Class 5 at even moderate water levels. The river narrows to a single channel and drops 8 feet over a boulder with a thin flow at the center and a boiling flume at each side. The fifth rapids is a series of 3 drops in rapid succession in a 20-foot channel. The bottom 2 have huge souse holes up against the undercut right shore. The remaining 3 ledges are straightforward rapids, the last of which can be reached from the take-out and is an excellent whitewater training site.

Due to the discharge of the Grafton dam, this can be "run" anytime, but if several gates are open, the whole narrow valley is a nightmare of explosion waves, *moving* 12- to 15-foot waves, and terrible souse holes. An interesting site from the railroad tracks, but no place for anyone's boat.

SHUTTLE: Valley Falls State Park is easily found by following the signs from either Fairmont or Grafton along WV 310 and CR 31/14 respectively. To reach the Hammond take-out, follow the yellow brick road (honest), "86," by turning off of WV 310.

GAUGE: The Grafton Dam has a gauge, but readings are meaningless to the authors. The above gauge reading is for Colfax. See section F below. Decision to run this can only be made after on-the-spot observations.

F. Hammond to Colfax—5 Miles

CLASS	GRADIENT	VOLUME	SCENERY	TIME	LEVEL
1,2–B	4(1@20)	2,547	A,C	1.5	0–3′

MAPS: USGS—Fairmont East and West
       COUNTY—Marion

DESCRIPTION: There are no danger spots on this run unless there are several gates open at the Grafton Dam. Normally a pleasant Class 1–2 run for 1 mile below the brickyard. Take the first island to the left and the rest on the right for the best rapids. The remaining 4 miles are fairly flat through attractive scenery. Take out at Colfax on the left just past the bridge or continue on to Fairmont for another 4.5 miles of flat water.

SHUTTLE: To get to Hammond, see section E, above. Colfax is on CR 66 west from WV 310 and north from Hammond.

GAUGE: Homemade gauge located on bridge support at Colfax. Has been run at 8 feet.

MIDDLE FORK RIVER

Adolph to US 33—16 Miles

MAPS: USGS—Adolph, Cassity, and Ellamore
COUNTIES—Randolph and Upshur

Not yet a river, the creek rushes along in fairly continuous Class 2 style. There is 1 short bouldery stretch below Cassity, then the river gradually flattens. The scenery includes a pretty wooded valley above Cassity, some unattractive mines at Cassity, and from Cassity to US 33, an interesting little canyon. From US 33 to Laurel Fork, the river is totally flat.

A. Laurel Fork to Audra State Park—5 Miles

CLASS	GRADIENT	VOLUME	SCENERY	TIME	LEVEL
1–3	26	330	A–B	1–2	3.5–6'

MAPS: USGS—Sago 15' and Audra
COUNTIES: Barbour and Upshur

DESCRIPTION: This interesting and lively little trout stream starts off quite tranquilly over Class 1 riffles past delightful little islands and then gradually changes character. The rapids become more numerous, more continuous, more complicated, and steeper. Passing the halfway mark, the paddler's view is obscured by numerous boulders and rock gardens, making this a thrilling Class 3 slalom course for the intermediate paddler. As the edge of the state park is reached, the intensity, but not the continuity, of the rapids lets up.

Once a beautiful wilderness river, the left-hand bank is currently undergoing "development" by real estate agents who have cut an ugly, landscarring road into the woods so that cabins, trailers, etc., may be located along the stream. One aspect that bears watching is a large oil or gas well installation uncomfortably close to the river.

DIFFICULTIES: There are no difficulties other than the possibility of broaching on the numerous boulders. One rapids at about halfway may appear choked, and locating the correct passage in lower water may be difficult. There are many 2- to 3-foot ledges in this run and 1 fairly vigorous 6- to 8-foot stairstep drop, but most are uncomplicated.

This run could be mean in very high water (over 6 feet). In general, the best passages, including around islands, are to the left. Do not run the last rapids under the bridge unless you plan to run section B since the area around this part of the river is fenced in. By the way, this rapids is much more difficult than anything above.

SHUTTLE: The take-out is immediately above the bridge. A parking lot is located on the right. To reach the put-in, take the road upstream that leaves the park on the left side of the river. This hardsurface road soon makes a sharp right toward Buckhannon, but a dirt road continues straight (to Mount Nebo) and should be taken. Soon this dirt road forks again. Take the left fork down the steep hillside to a clearing and another fork. Bear to the left; just past a vacation cabin there is a spot to park and easily launch the boats (known by the locals as "Finnegan's Ford"). This road continues upstream a considerable distance. A fast Class 1 run in high water may be made by putting in at a Boy Scout camp 5 miles above.

GAUGE: See Section B, below.

B. Audra State Park to Tygart Junction—6 Miles

CLASS	GRADIENT	VOLUME	SCENERY	TIME	LEVEL
4	2.5@79	330	A	3	3.5–5'

MAPS: USGS—Audra
COUNTY—Barbour

DESCRIPTION: Look at the rapids under the bridge at Audra State Park, look at the lush sylvan surroundings, subtract the road, bridge, and bathhouse, and then you'll know what to expect for the first 2.6 miles of this run. It's a beautiful, busy boat buster. The rapids under the bridge can be run on the right side, heading straight for the retaining wall of the swimming area, and then slipping to the left down into the pool when the water is low. When it is high, it is more entertaining to fandango down through the center. Beyond the pool you'll have to carefully pick channels for the next 60 minutes to the first of 3 major rapids above the mouth of the Middle Fork.

The river empties into the Tygart Gorge at about its midpoint. The only way out is to paddle the remaining 4 miles to the mouth of the Buckhannon. This results in an interesting 2 trips for the price of 1.

First there is the steep, rocky, technical paddling of the lower Middle Fork and then the much heavier, pushy Tygart with its tripled volume.

DIFFICULTIES: About an hour into the trip a hemlock-bedecked isle looms midstream. It cannot be run on the left except in high water. The right side is an interesting slide rapids with a stopper that tends to shunt the unwary into a left-side whirlpool. Several cycles are required before breakout. The big 3 rapids in the last half mile of the Middle Fork are next and will require scouting. The first is long and goes around a corner to the right after about 100 yards. The worst drop is before the turn. Enter in the middle and then paddle to the right. The next big rapids, recognized by a 50-foot boulder on the bottom left, looks bad on the right, but go there anyway because a broken ledge at the left bottom is terrible. Go to the right over high, clean ledges. The third and last rapids before the mouth can be run on the left where the water smashes into a high bank wall. Below that the water runs through an impassable sluice, and the boat must be scraped over the right-side wet slope and must then fall off a 2-foot ledge before running through the last drop and waves.

SHUTTLE: Audra State Park may be reached by "11" from either US 119 or 250. For the take-out, see the Tygart, section B. The ingeniously designed campgrounds at the state park offer the finest riverside camping of any place in West Virginia.

GAUGE: The government gauge just upstream from the bridge at Audra State Park has been partly washed away, but one can extrapolate to get a reading. The Belington gauge on the Tygart should be 4'+.

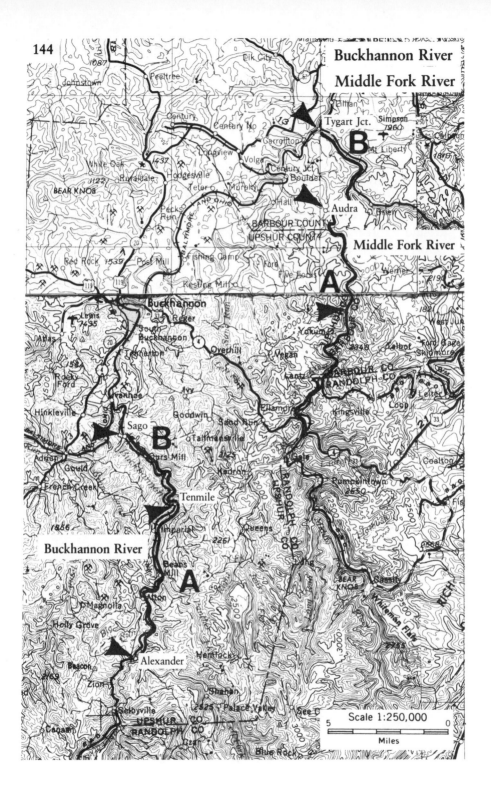

Buckhannon River

Middle Fork River

Middle Fork River

Buckhannon River

Scale 1:250,000

Miles

BUCKHANNON RIVER

A. Alexander to Tenmile—9 Miles

CLASS	GRADIENT	VOLUME	SCENERY	TIME	LEVEL
1–3	27	584	A–B	3	7–10'

MAPS: USGS—Alton
COUNTY—Upshur

DESCRIPTION: This is a deceptive river in that its extremely sluggish placidity below Buckhannon and its small size in the headwaters area near Alexander belie what is in store for the paddler between Alton (pronounced Elton by the locals) and Sago. The river begins at a very small scenic stream where the Right and Left forks join at Alexander. There is hardly anything more than straightforward riffles for 5 miles until one gets well below Alton. Here the gradient picks up to 40 fpm, and the rapids become complicated and closely spaced. Each rapids is fairly steep and, in low water, a good deal of tight maneuvering will be necessary. There are actually very few large sight-obstructing boulders, but vision is still limited by the gradient and the many bends in the river. All but the advanced paddler should arrange a take-out at Tenmile because the river's character changes drastically from there on. Since the best action is below Alton, most will not want to bother with the Alexander to Alton stretch.

DIFFICULTIES: There are none to speak of other than the usual difficulties encountered in rock garden types of rapids. Most of the rapids below Alton are 50- to 100-yard descents through such patches.

SHUTTLE: From Alexander take CR 11 west to WV 20, then right through Adrian to CR 22, then again right to Sago. Continue on CR 22 to CR 9 at Tallmansville. Turn right on "9" and proceed south to CR 9/8 and turn right to Tenmile. Alton may be reached via CR 11/15 and 32/14 from Alexander. See shuttle for section B, below.

GAUGE: See section B, below.

B. Tenmile to Sago—4 Miles

CLASS	GRADIENT	VOLUME	SCENERY	TIME	LEVEL
$3-5_6$	53	584	B	2	7–10'

MAPS: USGS—Buckhannon
        COUNTY—Upshur

DESCRIPTION: This is an isolated stretch of expert-level water on an unlikely river running through nineteenth-century Appalachia. It is one of the crude nuggets all good paddlers seek. The first 3 miles are very difficult and much scouting will be required. The last mile into Sago is fairly flat with comparatively minor rapids. New mining operations have marred a lot of the nice scenery.

DIFFICULTIES: Shortly below Tenmile the river pools behind a boulder-choked natural dam. The water flows primarily to the right side and seemingly sluices in a boulder-studded 15-foot channel at a right angle across to the left side; however, most of this sluice leaks out under 8-foot boulders from the downstream side, creating a very dangerous trap. In fact a paddler was trapped under and between the big boulders in 1970. Fortunately he was spit out of the current, but recent observations have shown various obstructing pieces of debris in this opening which could snag an underwater body. Avoid this Class 6 channel entirely and hop your boat down the secondary channel on the left side of this obstruction.

The river slides along over interesting rapids for a mile below this nightmare to the second bad rapids. This one is a long boulder-strewn slide complicated by an S-shaped entrance, which frequently results involuntarily in eddy turns. If this happens, the paddler should back down the rest of the rapids rather than chance broaching on the rapids-dividing, wet boulder halfway down.

The third meany eats boats on every trip and can be respected from the right-side portage. The river drops 3 feet through narrow passages at the top and then races over irregular rocks on a left slant to batter against an ugly shelf. This can sometimes be run as far left as possible, sneaking out a spot between 2 entrance boulders.

Beyond this the river slides and drops over innumerable ledges between and around sight-obstructing boulders. This is a Class 4 run without major problems until the rotted bridge piers of the ghost town of Ours Mills is reached, indicating the end of the action.

SHUTTLE: This is a dandy place to get lost. Sago, Alton, and Alexander can all be reached by hard roads from WV 20. Difficult, unmarked roads connect Sago with Tenmile, Tenmile with Alton, and Alton with Alexander, and all are very time-consuming. We would suggest a put-in at Alton and, for intermediates, a take-out at Tenmile. A final take-out for a 9-mile trip by river is located 1 mile above Sago. Finding Sago and Alton is no problem. Tenmile can be reached from Sago via Tallmansville by following our directions. If you try one of the "shortcuts," take plenty of gas, maps, and a flashlight. Read the shuttle for section A, above, with a copy of the Upshur County map handy.

GAUGE: There is a government gauge at Buckhannon. A reading can be obtained by calling (412) 644-2890. About 10 stones showing on the right abutment of the Alton bridge will ensure adequate water.

C. The Buckhannon Below Sago to Tygart River—36 Miles

MAPS: USGS—Buckhannon, Century, and Audra
        COUNTIES—Upshur and Barbour

Below Sago, the river winds placidly for 36 miles to Carrollton dropping only 2–3 fpm in the process. This part would make an excellent canoe-camping-fishing trip. Scenery gets pretty in one wild section near the entrance at Sand Run. The good whitewater section starts about a half mile above the covered bridge at Carrollton. This has been described under section C of the Tygart.

TRIBUTARIES OF THE BUCKHANNON RIVER

RIGHT FORK of Buchhannon River: Pickens to Selbyville—12 Miles

MAPS: USGS—Pickens and Goshen
        COUNTIES—Randolph and Upshur

This is a marginal run, even at high water. The first 3 miles to Silica are tiny and scrapy with occasional tree hazards. A decent-sized tributary makes boating at least reasonable from there on down. Not far past Silica is a small island, below which is an imposing, tilting, double ledge (3 feet, 6 feet). Afterward, there are a few other small ledges, then nonstop whitewater (Class 3) to Selbyville. There is a 6-foot dam at a camp at Selbyville; carry on the left. The river is much slower below here.

LEFT FORK OF RIGHT FORK of Buckhannon River: Helvetia to Selbyville—17 Miles

MAPS: USGS—Pickens
        COUNTIES—Randolph and Upshur

Lovely run. The water is fairly clear, and at first follows the road. After Czar it flows through a narrow, uninhabited valley. The whitewater is continuous and builds up to a bouncy run over submerged boulders (Class 3).

LEFT FORK of Buckhannon River: Helvetia-Adolph Road to Junction of Right Fork of Buckhannon—8 Miles

MAPS: USGS—Pickens and Alton
        COUNTIES—Randolph and Upshur

This is nonstop, easy (Class 2–3) whitewater over an even gradient. There are 2 low-water railroad bridges requiring carries. The scenery consists of a pretty, wooded canyon marred by some road scars, a few cabins, and a mine vent.

THREE FORK CREEK

Near WV 92 to Thornton — 12 Miles

CLASS	GRADIENT	VOLUME	SCENERY	TIME	LEVEL
	2@30				
1–4	1.5@60	S	B–C	3	0–6″

MAPS: USGS — Thornton, Gladesville, and Newburg
COUNTIES — Preston and Taylor

DESCRIPTION: This is a very small stream that can only be run when there has been a lot of rain. The water is very acidic, the rocks orange, and the scenery poor in many places, but it has some very interesting rapids. The upper 2 miles below WV 92 are steep and can only be run when the water is very high. Runs may also start at a bridge on the Gladesville-Independence road "33." The scenery here is very attractive as the laurel and hemlock crowd in on the stream, but the water is fairly flat with only occasional riffles. As the water begins picking up speed and complexity, the next bridge is met, which ends this 3-mile segment and is the signal for the beginning of the Class 3–4, action-packed 1.5 miles. In this latter section, there are 3 falls.

After passing the third falls, the water tapers off to a Class 2 for another 2 miles. You might consider taking out at the second bridge beyond the last falls. The water below here to Thornton is fairly fast but contains very few riffles. Paddling beyond Thornton is not recommended as the water is even flatter, the scenery uninteresting, and very few opportunities for take-outs exist.

DIFFICULTIES: Just before, under, and beyond the second bridge from the put-in is Victoria Falls, a steep slide rapids into very turbulent water and then over a 2- to 4-foot ledge into a powerful hydraulic. The rapids after this are all closely spaced, steep, and complex. The second and third falls are near the end of this 1.5-mile course. The first of these, Yosemite, is a steep staircase descent taken on the right and the next rapids, the third falls (Niagara), is a riverwide shelf with several passages. Scouting is recommended for the first and third falls. The falls have been given these grand names not only for the power they connote, but also to bring a suggestion of beauty to this otherwise forlorn land.

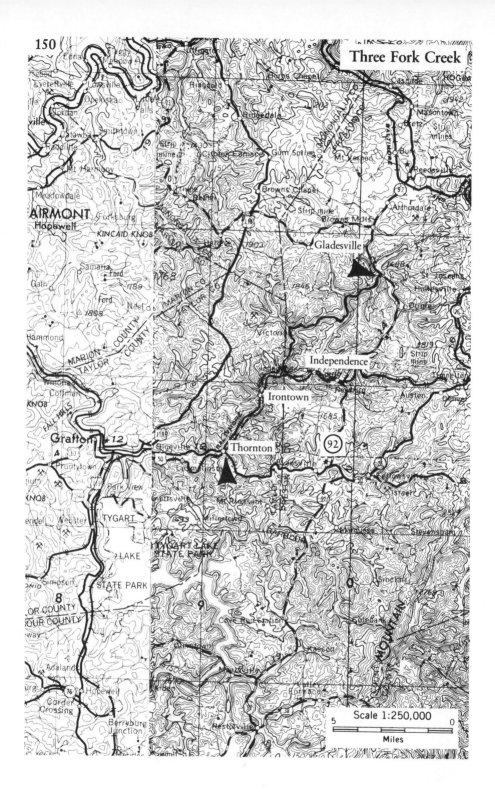

Scale 1:250,000

Miles

SHUTTLE: Put in at the first bridge below WV 92 on the Three Fork Creek Road "35," or at the bridge next to the tavern on "33," 2.5 miles south of Gladesville. Continue on this road to Independence and bear right following the road to Doortown. Take-outs can be made at the bridge there, the next one downstream at Irontown, or under the US 50 bridge at Thornton. For nothing but action, put in at the Victoria Falls bridge reached by taking the road next to the cemetery from Gladesville. Take out under the power line right-of-way below the last falls if no one is around. The people owning the property just upstream from here get pretty uptight about this though so it would be better to paddle another half mile down to the Doortown bridge.

GAUGE: There is a canoeing gauge at the bridge south of Gladesville, but no experience has been gained with the river at really high levels. The zero is very liberal, however, and was set to indicate scraping on the first ledge at Victoria Falls. It can be run a lot lower than this with a lift over that ledge.

WHITEDAY CREEK

Camp Calico to Monongahela River—9 Miles

CLASS	GRADIENT	VOLUME	SCENERY	TIME	LEVEL
	3@55				
1–3	6@23	S	B	3	1–3'

MAPS: USGS—Rivesville
       COUNTIES—Monongalia and Marion

DESCRIPTION: This anxious little screamer forms the Monongalia-Marion county line. The first 2 miles are continuous Class 3 with no pools and very few eddies. This has been compared to a small Savage River, and a road runs alongside for an abbreviated run. The second or middle part down to WV 73 consists of more open Class 2 water, while the final 3 miles consist of mainly big waves and ledges up to Class 3. The stream is only 20–40 feet wide. The tiny steep section above the put-in has been run during a very high-water period, but it's filthy with trees.

DIFFICULTIES: In the first quarter of a mile there is a left-hand bend against an auto-sized boulder. Stay to the right of center to avoid another partially submerged rock in the bend. You can eddy out immediately to pick up paddlers, etc. Several islands and fallen trees invigorate the next 2 miles. The dam below the WV 73 bridge strangely enough no longer exists; it washed out.

SHUTTLE: Take "79" east from CR 73 at the golf course and turn right at a sign identifying Camp Calico. Put in at the pool above the bridge. Alternatively, all of the roads turning right from "79" reach Whiteday Creek or CR 73/1 which parallels the creek. From "73/1" you can drive up- or downstream to find a put-in as water level permits. To reach the take-out, take "36" from CR 73 at Smithtown and proceed to the third bridge over these troubled waters, a half mile short of the Opekiska Locks.

GAUGE: There are gauges on the WV 73 bridge on a right-side rock just below and on the first bridge downstream along "36." All are similar in the paddling range. The downstream gauge will likely be up after a heavy winter rain. A 0.5 reading is adequate for playing on the 3 miles below WV 73.

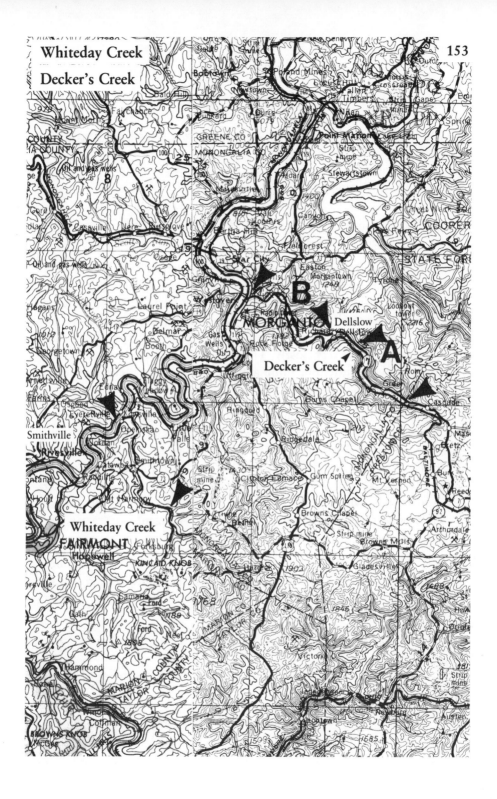

DECKER'S CREEK

A. Preston-Monongalia County Line to WV 7 Bridge—5 Miles

CLASS	GRADIENT	VOLUME	SCENERY	TIME	LEVEL
$2-3_6$	40(1@200!)	99	A–C	1	$1'+$

MAPS: USGS—Masontown and Morgantown South
　　　　COUNTY—Monongalia

DESCRIPTION: This is the only whitewater stream that Monongalia County owns all by itself, and it's a humdinger. After a put-in just below an unrunnable cascade of successive waterfalls, it moves right along at a fast small-stream, Class 3 pace through dense laurel thickets, ledges, fallen logs, and low-hanging branches. It is a very rocky stream and follows WV 7 very closely. The scenery gets crudded up as it passes through 2 large limestone mining areas, and one must actually paddle through culverts at these places.

DIFFICULTIES: Watch out for downed trees, trapped debris, and a possible clogged culvert. At high water 3 bridges at Greer are too low to go under. Other than these ordinary dangers, all you need worry about is the 200 fpm drop to the WV 7 bridge at Pioneer Rocks, a so far unrunnable "Class 7" rapids. It is one horrendous drop after another for a whole mile. You could be hurt real bad if you goofed. The second half has been run a few times by Morgantown crazy types, but boats and bodies are always getting damaged.

SHUTTLE: Park at the county line on WV 7 for a fairly gentle slope to the put-in. Take out somewhere above the highway sign HILL. Perhaps it should read HELL, as this marks the start of the Pioneer Rocks section.

GAUGE: Refers to the Dellslow bridge. See section B, below.

B. Dellslow at WV 7 Bridge to Monongahela River—6 Miles

CLASS	GRADIENT	VOLUME	SCENERY	TIME	LEVEL
1–3	28 2@50	99	D	2	0–2′

MAPS: USGS—Morgantown North and South
COUNTY—Monongalia

DESCRIPTION: Once one of the most beautiful streams in northern West Virginia, this little stream is now polluted with strip mine acids, crushed limestone, industrial pollutants, and raw sewage. The scenery is terrible—one literally canoes through the bowels of Morgantown— but there's plenty of action for late winter canoeing.

DIFFICULTIES: Within 25 yards of the put-in there is a 4-foot S-turn ledge which is Class 3 at medium water. The first 2 miles drop 104 feet with most of that occurring in the first mile. Several hazards line the way. At mile 1 the broken-down bridge at Richard may be choked with debris. Later, after turning the corner below the bridge at Rock Forge, one enters a long, sterile channel built by the Department of Highways to replace the river they bulldozed aside. As one approaches the large factory on the right there is a dangerous fall consisting of very sharp boulders left behind by the construction. Scout for the best passage since you can't afford to hit these sharp rocks. One may need to carry the low-water bridge at Marilla Park if the water is high. At mile 5 the river drops sharply over a series of ledges and heads under a high overpass. The water gets up to Class 3 and turns sharply to the right through high-standing waves. The left-hand "bank" is a concrete wall. Just below this there is another ledge which must be run on the far left in a tight passage between the bank and a fallen tree; the final ledge is a few hundred yards below this and should be scouted to find the best passage. The biggest danger on this run would be an upset. It would be helpful to invite the Tidy Bowl man to paddle with you.

SHUTTLE: Put in just above the WV 7 bridge at Dellslow. Take-out can be reached by paddling down the Monongahela under the Westover bridge, being careful to dodge the spit from the playful urchins above, and taking out at the foot of Walnut Street 1 block beyond the bridge.

GAUGE: None. The top of the right footing of the Dellslow bridge can be considered zero.

OTHER STREAMS OF THE TYGART SUB-BASIN

LAUREL CREEK: WV 38 to Tygart River—5.5 Miles

MAPS: USGS—Nestorville
Monongahela National Forest
COUNTY—Barbour

This cleverly named torrent affords a 5.5-mile run that evolves from placid to thrilling. The cruise starts with a relaxing 2.5-mile float through a mostly wooded, gorgelike valley marred only by a few mining scars. There are many riffles and uncomplicated rapids. Passing the first road bridge the gradient begins growing, and rounded sandstone boulders form long and complex rapids. This is great fun and thrilling, but it can only be considered a warm-up exercise if the final mile from the second road bridge down to the Tygart is on your itinerary. Rapids build to greater and greater steepness and complexity, climaxing in a memorable stretch that begins with a steep boulder rapids which piles into a big, nightmarish "floating" boulder with about half the river flowing underneath it (Class 6). Next are 2 huge sloping ledges, which are, in turn, followed by a 10-foot falls runnable on the extreme right and 2 short but intense and exacting boulder piles. If you survive all that, you have made it to the Tygart. Congratulate yourself.

SHUTTLE: Take WV 38 east to WV 92. Turn left and go 3 miles to CR 10 and left to Moatsville. Follow the road up the Tygart 2.7 miles to Laurel Creek.

GAUGE: None.

TETER CREEK: Nestorville to Tygart River—4 Miles

MAPS: USGS—Nestorville
Monongahela National Forest
COUNTY—Barbour

Teensy Teter Creek tumbles into the Tygart near Moatsville in Barbour County, West Virginia. This is only a 1.5-mile run unless you start at WV 38 at Nestorville, which we recommend just for its warm-up value. The first mile is a relatively easy float over lots of mildly dropping boulder gardens and little ledges. Just above the bridge in

Moatsville is a strikingly massive sloping ledge formation negotiable via a long, pushy, complex route on the right. If this bothers you, then take out right there. The rest of the way tilts at up to 120 feet per mile through narrow slots, around blind bends, and against and beneath menacing undercuts in a beautiful bouldery environment. And just to keep things interesting, all this is garnished by an occasional ill-placed strainer or two. The Tygart will look like the Mississippi when and if you arrive at the take-out.

SHUTTLE: WV 92 and CR 10 parallel the creek.

GAUGE: None.

SANDY CREEK: WV 92 to Tygart Lake—8 Miles

MAPS: USGS—Thornton
        COUNTIES—Barbour, Taylor, and Preston

Actually this is 2 runs, the first part recommended for the novice and the second for the advanced paddler. The creek from WV 92 to the second road bridge (Hiram) is mostly flat but has a swift current and even occasional riffles. It twists through an attractive gorge-like valley past mostly wooded slopes, some fields, and only an occasional house. Below Hiram, roads and civilization depart the stream as it roars downhill to the Tygart. The whitewater varies from easy boulder patches to ledges to steep boulder dams. The final plunge into Tygart Lake is the most formidable rapids on the river, resembling a piece out of the upper Yough. Now comes the time to pay for all your fun, with a 2.5-mile paddle up the lake to a roadhead at the mouth of Big Cove Run. (One obviously wants to know the level of the lake when planning this.) This is the most convenient spot to shuttle to for those putting in at WV 92. Those running the lower creek only would do well to check out the road, CR 48, to the mouth of Frog Run about 2 miles downlake.

SHUTTLE: Via WV 92 and CR 2 west to Cove Run. See also the shuttle for section D of the Tygart.

GAUGE: None.

WEST FORK RIVER: Walkersville to Ben Dale—21 Miles

MAPS: USGS—Walkersville and Roanoke
       COUNTY—Lewis

DESCRIPTION: This is generally an attractive stream, but most of this section will be lost to Stonewall Jackson Dam. Above Roanoke it meanders, small and sluggish, along a roomy, green pastoral valley, with low banks affording good views of the scenery. The valley is sparsely populated, and roads and railroads are usually not to be seen. As the river gets larger it flows through woodlands, then rugged pasture-covered hills, then more woods. Most houses on the lower river have been leveled for the lake.

DIFFICULTIES: These include trees and snags; a low-water bridge below Walkersville; 2 collapsed, low wooden bridges below Roanoke; a 2.5-foot dam with a strong roller under a green pipe bridge about 2 miles below Roanoke; and an 8-foot dam at the take-out. (Carry right.)

DUNKARD CREEK

MAPS: USGS—Blacksville and Osage
       COUNTY—Monongalia

This is a very long, winding stream that parallels the Mason-Dixon line through northern Monongalia County. Its mouth is on the Monongahela in Pennsylvania. Parts of it have been run by canoe. Float fishing in rowboats is popular. In high water there is little more than Class 1 riffles. The stream is very rich in waterfowl, and bass and muskie fishing is especially good. It could be run from as far west as Blacksville all the way to Mt. Morris, Pennsylvania. Although the road distance between bridges may be short, the river distance may be twice as far due to its meandering qualities.

4 The Northwest Quadrant— The Ohio Basin

Although this section of the state is hilly enough, the rivers do not have sufficient gradient to create any significant whitewater. The land is sparsely populated and rural in character. Much of the scenery is farms and second-growth timber. Rivers here are lined by mud banks and sand beaches with rare outcroppings of rocks. Some huge sycamores and other hardwood trees can be found along the river bottoms.

Fishing is a popular pastime, with bass, catfish, panfish, and some muskies to be found. Many of the largest muskies in the state are caught from Little Kanawha and Middle Island Creek.

Historically this area was the birthplace of the chemical and petroleum industries in this country. Many old, abandoned, shallow oil wells dot the countryside while the associated structures and access roads have almost been reclaimed by nature. Brine wells in the Ohio River Valley spawned Semet-Solveys (FMC), Union Carbide, and other industrial concerns which are now prominent in the Ohio-Kanawha River area.

The most famous resident of this area was pioneer hero Lewis Wetzel who among other things used to *run* between Morgantown and Wheeling (all the way) and would think nothing of swimming over to Ohio in the winter. Sort of West Virginia's Davy Crockett.

LITTLE KANAWHA RIVER

The Little Kanawha starts as a small trout stream in the mountains of southern Upshur County. It is here, below Route 20, that the only real whitewater section exists. It is a too small stream that can be run only in very high water and, even then, extremely critical maneuvering is required. Several rapids also must be carried, making this a run only for radical paddlers desperate for new rivers. Next, it cuts across a small section of Lewis County where it first becomes big enough to really run just before entering Braxton County. Except for 1 ledge at Falls Mill the journey across Braxton, Gilmer, Calhoun, Wirt, and Wood counties is rather uneventful. Scenery is generally pastoral, and

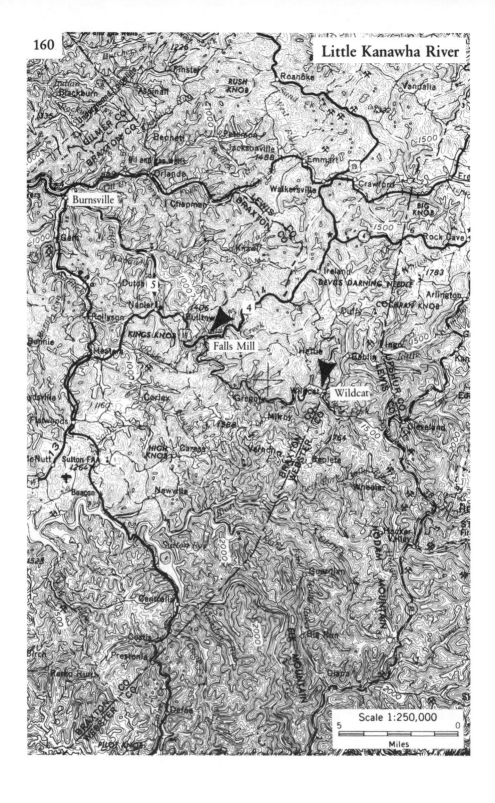

Scale 1:250,000

5   0

Miles

the river is slow-flowing and bounded by mud banks. This also seems to be the poison ivy capital of the world. Remnants of several turn-of-the-century locks exist, one of which, Well's Locks below Elizabeth, must be carried.

Wildcat to Falls Mill—13 Miles

CLASS	GRADIENT	VOLUME	SCENERY	TIME	LEVEL
C-1$_4$	10	274	A–B	4	NA

MAPS: USGS—Orlando, Newville, and Hacker Valley
       COUNTIES—Lewis and Braxton

DESCRIPTION: This is good for novices in winter or early spring when the water is up. The entire trip is remote and scenic. Don't expect much in the way of rapids, especially in high water. The gradient allows no more than Class 1 riffles. There is a lot of flat water, but it moves along at a good flow. The pool below the falls has been a popular fishin' and swimmin' hole for generations.

DIFFICULTIES: There is only one and it is a real lulu—the falls that gives the hamlet at the take-out its name. Novices can easily take out above the falls while the more experienced may want to run it. There is nothing to it actually, just over the top, down over the steep drop, and into an almost keeper-sized hydraulic. Perfectly straightforward.

SHUTTLE: Use WV 4 from Falls Mill east to Ireland and turn right on "50" to Wildcat.

GAUGE: None. If water is 6 inches below the footing of the Wildcat bridge, there will be plenty of water. An easier place for observation is the Falls Mill bridge, where a reading of 6.5 stones down on the right upstream is adequate.

Burnsville to Grantsville—40 Miles

MAPS: USGS—Burnsville, Gilmer, Glenville, Tanner, and Grantsville
       COUNTIES—Braxton, Gilmer, and Calhoun

The pool of the Burnsville dam starts just below the take-out of the Falls Mill run, but the river is basically flat anyway. This run is pretty bland, with minimal current and scenery of rolling woods and pasture marred by a few mining operations.

Grantsville to WV 5 Bridge Below Bigbend—11 Miles

MAPS: USGS—Grantsville and Annamoriah
       COUNTY—Calhoun

A short, very popular fishing trip, this section of the river detours from most civilization for 5 miles when it departs from the road about 2 miles below Grantsville. Impressive stringers of bass caught from this section are not unusual.

WV 5 Below Bigbend to Creston—15 Miles

MAPS: USGS—Annamoriah and Burning Springs
       COUNTIES—Calhoun and Wirt

This is also known as the Annamoriah to Creston run since Annamoriah is slightly closer than Bigbend to the WV 5 bridge. The put-in is generally made along CR 1 to Industry, which is located 1.2 miles east of the WV 5 bridge. From Industry to Creston is 8 miles, from WV 5 to Creston, 14. Choose the distance you like and settle back for the most pleasant section on the river. The scenery is remote and probably the prettiest on the Little Kanawha. The shuttle is easy; just follow WV 5 across the mountain between Annamoriah and Creston. The river forms a large bend so the shuttle is only 4 miles.

Sanoma to Burning Springs—4.5 Miles

MAPS: USGS—Burning Springs
       COUNTY—Wirt

WV 5 follows the river most of the way from Creston to Sanoma. Sanoma is located on "36," 4 miles west of Creston, and can be the put-in for a short 4.5-mile, reasonably remote trip. Watch out for the low-water bridge at Sanoma in high water because it forms a very bad hydraulic at the right water level.

Sanoma is somewhat unique in that a ferry was in operation as late as the 1950s. In the summer, when the Little Kanawha gets down to a trickle, the operator tied his boat in the center of the river and dropped a ramp to each bank. Then he charged a fee to drive across the boat à la toll bridge.

The take-out at Burning Springs may be made along WV 5 when the river returns to the road, or along "35/9" which runs a short distance upstream from Burning Springs.

Burning Springs to Parkersburg—37 Miles

MAPS: USGS—Burning Springs, Girta, Elizabeth, Kanawha, South
               Parkersburg, and Parkersburg
           COUNTIES—Wirt and Wood

The river is basically flat with little current as it flows toward the Ohio River. Eight miles below Elizabeth the Hughes River joins in but adds little except more of the same. The last 12 miles are Ohio River backwater.

LITTLE KANAWHA TRIBUTARIES

MAPS: USGS—Peniel, Reedy, Burning Springs, Arnoldsburg, and
               Spencer
           COUNTIES—Calhoun, Roane, and Wirt

Many small- to medium-size tributaries of the Little Kanawha are runnable in periods of high runoff. These all have similar characteristics—mud banks, shallow riffles, long pools, fallen trees. Four of the larger streams are the West Fork and Beech Fork of the Little Kanawha, Spring Creek, and Reedy Creek. The West Fork starts in Calhoun County and joins with the Beech Fork at the Roane County line. Reedy Creek and Spring Creek both begin in Roane County, and all of these streams then flow into Wirt County to join the Little Kanawha between Creston and Palestine.

HUGHES RIVER

The Hughes River drainage is made up of 3 main watersheds, its North and South forks and Goose Creek. In general, there are highways and summer camps close by except for the segments described below. Scenery is pastoral, lightly populated, slightly trashy, and with frequent high mud banks which prevent seeing much of anything anyway.

The South Fork is runnable from Smithville. WV 47 parallels the river all of the way so scouting and shuttle can be done easily and at the same time. At Cisco, the North Fork enters, doubling the volume of the river. From this point, the Hughes River proper flows 12.5 miles to its confluence with the Little Kanawha. Goose Creek comes in from the right halfway down, adding significant flow.

In very high water, the North Fork may be paddled from as high as Toll Gate on US 50. From there to Cairo it flows through relatively isolated country with heavily wooded and steep-sided valleys. At Cairo the scenery takes a step down, but after a mile or so it returns to peaceful surroundings. Below Cairo, CR 15 is fairly close to the river. This continues to the junction with the South Fork at Cisco.

Harrisville to Cairo—14 Miles

MAPS: USGS—Harrisville and Cairo
        COUNTY—Ritchie

This section has not been paddled as far as we know, but it has been scouted and is easily large enough for an enjoyable trip in the winter and spring or after heavy local rains. The riverbed is 30–60 feet wide in a narrow-walled and heavily wooded valley. There is no significant gradient, but there is fair current most of the way. The watercourse is mostly secluded, but some civilization is seen around the camping areas of North Bend State Park. Downstream a few hundred yards from the first campground is a low concrete dam that has rubble and trees below and should probably be portaged. Watch for it.

The entire trip is 14 miles but could easily be divided in half at the first campground on CR 5. The shuttle can be made from the WV 16 bridge 1 mile north of Harrisville to the WV 31 bridge in Cairo by taking WV 16 to Harrisville and then WV 31 to Cairo, or alternatively taking "5" out of Harrisville to North Bend and then "14" to Cairo. Turn right on WV 31 from "14" when reaching Cairo.

GOOSE CREEK

Petroleum to Freeport—10 Miles

CLASS	GRADIENT	VOLUME	SCENERY	TIME	LEVEL
1	20	S	B+	2.5	NA

MAPS: USGS—Petroleum
COUNTIES—Ritchie and Wirt

DESCRIPTION: Scenery is fairly attractive even though the railroad crosses the creek 4 times in the first couple of miles below Petroleum. Numerous rock walls and ledges are encountered, along with some very small side streams with attractive waterfalls. Current is fast and waves are small.

SHUTTLE: Take-out is below the WV 47 bridge in Freeport where Goose Creek joins the Hughes. The shuttle from Freeport to Petroleum is 9 miles via WV 47, CR 15, and CR 11. Go east from Freeport to Cisco, where you turn left on CR 15. There is an arrow pointing toward Hughes River Public Hunting Area and a sign "to Cairo." CR 11 is the second left, 1.4 miles from WV 47. Put-in can be made at Petroleum, or turn right on CR 18 toward Nutter Farm and put in at Myers Fork, 1.6 miles upstream.

GAUGE: None

Scale 1:250,000

Miles

MILL CREEK

Above Statts Mills—7 Miles

MAPS: USGS—Kentuck
         COUNTY—Jackson

Mill Creek offers almost 35 miles of pleasant flat-water paddling.

The most scenic and also the smallest section is the headwater section of the Tug Fork of Mill Creek called Grass Lick. This can be seen from I-77 near Fairplain, although it is too small to paddle until Stone Lick joins it. Put-in may be reached by turning south on US 21 from I-77 at Fairplain and then turning left on Grass Lick Road. Follow this road until it turns to gravel and then to where it fords Grass Lick. If there is too much water to ford the creek, there is enough to paddle. Take-out may be made at Statts Mills, once the site of a covered bridge. Find Statts Mills by going north on US 21 from I-77 at Fairplain for about 100 yards, turn right on CR 21/26 for 0.4 mile, then left on CR 25 to the top of the hill, where you turn right on CR 36, Statts Mills Road. Go to the iron bridge. Total trip by water is 7 miles. Trip by road is only 10.5 miles but will seem at least twice that.

Statts Mills to Ripley—11.5 Miles

MAPS: USGS—Ripley
         COUNTY—Jackson

From Statts Mills to Ripley, Tug Fork Road follows the creek. A low-water bridge is out below Statts Mills, preventing you from crossing, so you have to go back out to CR 25. This section will soon have a flood-control dam because the interstate has blocked part of the floodplain in which the creek used to flow, leaving Mill Creek backed up around the Ripley interchange of I-77. A brilliant piece of makework.

Ripley to Ohio River—16 Miles

MAPS: USGS—Ripley and Cottageville
         COUNTY—Jackson

Below Ripley the scenery is civilized but not too bad. The broad valley around Evans and Cottageville is actually quite pretty. The last 6 miles or so are backwater from the Ohio, so you have to watch for powerboats.

OTHER STREAMS OF THE NORTHWEST QUADRANT

WHEELING AND LITTLE WHEELING CREEKS

MAPS: USGS—Wheeling
      COUNTY—Ohio

These streams which barge their way through beautiful downtown Wheeling aren't much to look at, but they are capable of coming up quickly, causing property damage, and loss of life. They definitely have whitewater (actually brown), and Wheeling Creek occasionally gets rafted by college students; but low-water bridges and interstate construction have added formidable hazards to any attempted run.

MIDDLE ISLAND CREEK: Sherwood to Ohio River—73+ Miles

MAPS: USGS—West Union, Shirley, Middlebourne, Paden City, Bens Run and Raven Rock
      COUNTIES—Doddridge, Tyler, and Pleasants

This is northern West Virginia's most popular float-fishing stream, yielding lunker-sized muskies. It winds for miles through Doddridge, Tyler, and Pleasants counties and has its mouth at Saint Marys. This is a big creek, 612 cfs average.

One really unique feature that makes Middle Island Creek stand out among West Virginia streams is "The Jug," a combination natural and man-made phenomenon whereby the creek traverses a 4-mile loop to return 100 feet from the put-in. This is made possible by a 9-foot-high low-water bridge (possibly a record) which spans and dams a very narrow notch through an equally narrow ridge. The creek is forced around a balloon-shaped peninusula only to return to the original bed just a few boat lengths downstream. The circuitous route is densely vegetated and some tree dodging must be done; however, the course is generally easy with good current. Take-out is at the put-in. (Or is the put-in at the take-out?) The Jug is located just east of Middlebourne on WV 18. Look for a restaurant—a beer joint called The Jug on a bend in the road. The real "Jug" is directly behind it, if you're walking straight.

POCATALICO RIVER

MAPS: USGS—Walton, Kettle, Romance, Sissonsville, Pocatalico,
and Saint Albans
COUNTIES—Roane, Kanawha, and Putnam

The Pocatalico River, known locally as the Poca, is a small, meandering, flat-water stream that is generally characterized by long pools alternating with short riffles. In the winter and early spring, it can be run from the vicinity of Walton in Roane County to its junction with the Kanawha River at Poca (a 50-mile run). There is almost always a road near the river, although the section below Walton to Cicerone is admittedly pretty low-grade road. Fishing is good for bass and muskie, although this stream does not seem a particularly popular spot.

If you wish to paddle a section of the river, first consult a set of county road maps. Often the road along the river is not well marked, particularly by the headwaters where the best scenery and fishing are found.

5   And a Couple from Neighboring States

Although this is supposed to be a comprehensive guide to the rivers of West Virginia, it doesn't seem right not to include 2 outstanding rivers from nearby states for several reasons. First of all, whitewater sport knows no political boundaries, and second, the 2 rivers in question, the Youghiogheny and the Savage, are paddled extensively by West Virginia paddlers. And what the heck—they are West Virginia rivers anyway, what with the headwaters of the Yough arising in our Preston County and it being a part of the Monongahela Basin and with the Savage being right on the state line and being a part of the Potomac system and all.

The Yough is probably the most oft-paddled river in the East, being supplied from a large reservoir through the dry summer months and also close to large population centers. At least 4 commercial firms sponsor raft or float trips on it, and it has long been the site of racing events and slalom training camps. It can be mean and brutal in high water and has taken the lives of several nonpaddlers in recent years. It is one of the prime recreational meccas of the state of Pennsylvania and is known nationwide among paddlers. The Yough is right in the midst of George Washington Country. In fact George was probably the first white paddler on the Yough, having explored the Confluence-to-Ohiopyle run in 1754. The word has come down that George didn't want to tackle the Loop.

The Savage is a river comparatively new to the paddling game, probably having first been paddled in 1968. It too is a dam-controlled river, but the reservoir is not large enough to accommodate summer-round paddling. The river has become famous as a site of slalom and wildwater races, and the first Olympic tryouts were attracted there in July 1972. Numerous U.S. Team Trials, national championships, and North American cup races have been held since. It is a river characterized by very big water in a very small streambed and has been the single most important reason that the quality of serious whitewater paddling has improved so much in the East in recent years.

YOUGHIOGHENY RIVER

A. Sang Run to Friendsville—10.5 Miles

CLASS	GRADIENT	VOLUME	SCENERY	TIME	LEVEL
	48				
4–5	3.5@116	632	A	5	1.9–2.8'

MAPS: USGS—Sang Run and Friendsville
COUNTY—Garrett, Maryland

DESCRIPTION: Below Sang Run bridge there are 3 miles of flat water to warm-up riffle and then Gap Falls, which is run on the left. One mile of Class 3 water follows and then the Bastard— start in the middle and get to the right avoiding a left terminal hole. Next is a complex 3-part rapids called Charlie's Choice, followed by another Triple Drop—Snaggle Tooth, Middle Drop, and National Falls (run left). Stay right to avoid Tommy's Hole, then run a left diagonal stopper with a house-size boulder in the center requiring a quick right turn. The latter is called Zinger. After a series of ledges, stay away from the right to run the heavy 4-foot Heinzerling Falls. A choice bit of mayhem, called Meat Cleaver, awaits the paddler downstream. Though not exceedingly difficult, this rapids is potentially very dangerous. Start down the right channel and cut close behind the left-hand boulder, being careful not to eddy out unintentionally. Then fly over the second drop either on the far left or "in the middle" (difficult to judge), in order to avoid 2 nasty midstream rocks which can't be seen from above. Powerful Popper is next, a great place to play. After a few playful sideways surfing holes come Lost and Found. There is a tombstone midstream. Lost is on the left, Found is on the right. Cheeseburger Falls should be run on the left. Dosido is the right side of Cheeseburger. After a series of moderate hydraulics follows Wright's Hole. Sneak it on the right middle, or plan to spend a week in it on the left, or swim through Double Pencil Sharpener next downstream.

The paddler has now come 3.5 miles from Gap Falls. Ahead are 4 miles of anticlimax.

DIFFICULTIES: Are you kidding?

SHUTTLE: Leave the take-out car at Friendsville. Drive south on

MD 42 for 5 miles. Turn right at a green trailer on the left, then take next turn to the right to Sang Run.

GAUGE: The above readings refer to a gauge painted on the bridge at Sang Run. There is a USGS gauge in Friendsville reported daily by the Pittsburgh National Weather Service, (412) 644-2890. It might prove useful for setting up a weekend trip in high-water season. Try for something around 3 feet on the Friendsville gauge.

B. Confluence to Ohiopyle — 10 Miles

CLASS	GRADIENT	VOLUME	SCENERY	TIME	LEVEL
1–2	10	1,899	A	3.5	1.7–4'

MAPS: USGS—Confluence 15'
Pennsylvania state road map

DESCRIPTION: This good run for novices or intermediates passes through a beautiful winding gorge. If there is not enough discharge from the dam, put in downstream beyond the mouth of the Casselman. For about 2 miles below the dam, there are only occasional riffles, with flat water predominating. About a mile below the outskirts of town, the river turns away from the broad valley and heads left into narrow confines. The first of several Class 2 rapids begins here. These are all easily read and delightful to run. Soon the rapids recede and the river broadens out considerably for 3 or 4 miles. If it is a windy day, this section can be painfully arduous (the wind *always* blows upstream for some reason). Soon, however, the canyon walls begin to squeeze the river in and rapids reform for the last 3 miles of the trip. Aside from the railroad tracks on either side, the river flows through a road-less, peopleless setting.

DIFFICULTIES: When you see the first signs of Ohiopyle in the distance on the right bank, you should begin to plan your approach. The more conservative paddlers will want to hang to the left of the island above the Ohiopyle bridge and land on the rocky "beach" just below it. More experienced paddlers will want to run the more difficult passages to the right and take out at either side of the bridge. In water under 2 feet, an upset at this point is not serious; all one has to do is stand up and walk to shore. Nonetheless, a take-out in Ohiopyle should always be made with caution and respect for the inexperienced members of the group due to the falls immediately below. Do not paddle beyond the railroad bridge.

SHUTTLE: Put in on the left side of the river in Confluence, anywhere from the Corps of Engineers recreation area on downstream for 2 miles. Heading back to Ohiopyle, take the first right beyond the cemetery.

GAUGE: See section C, below.

C. Ohiopyle to Stewarton—7 Miles

CLASS	GRADIENT	VOLUME	SCENERY	TIME	LEVEL
	1@100				
2–3	6@13	2,494	A	3	1.7–4'

MAPS: USGS—Confluence 15'
    Pennsylvania state road map

DESCRIPTION: The first mile of this section, known as the Loop, is the most popular and contains a great deal of action. The paddler has everything thrown at him but the kitchen sink. For openers, after putting in below the falls, the paddler must face the series of ledges known as Entrance Rapids without any warm-up. It is a long, tortuous course into twisted currents. For indiscretions, a huge rock (Sugarloaf) stands in mid-river as a sentinel to broach paddlerless boats or even paddled boats. Half of the upsets on the Loop take place here. Most paddlers stick to the left and regroup in an eddy below Entrance to mend boats, bandage bodies, retrieve paddles, and gather courage for the next rapids, Cucumber.

A long rock garden precedes an extremely vigorous drop through a narrow passage. Usually you should stick to the far left, carefully avoiding anything resembling a broaching situation, and gradually move to the right where huge boulders have forced the course of the river. The best advice from here is to hang on and keep your reflexive and anticipatory braces ready. Going through Cucumber with or without a boat is what it must be like to be flushed down the john.

The next rapids is merely a minor surfing hydraulic divided in midstream by a boulder. Following is an interesting drop into an S-shaped curler. After this there is a long, steep rock garden which can be run in a variety of ways. The far right is the most direct except for an

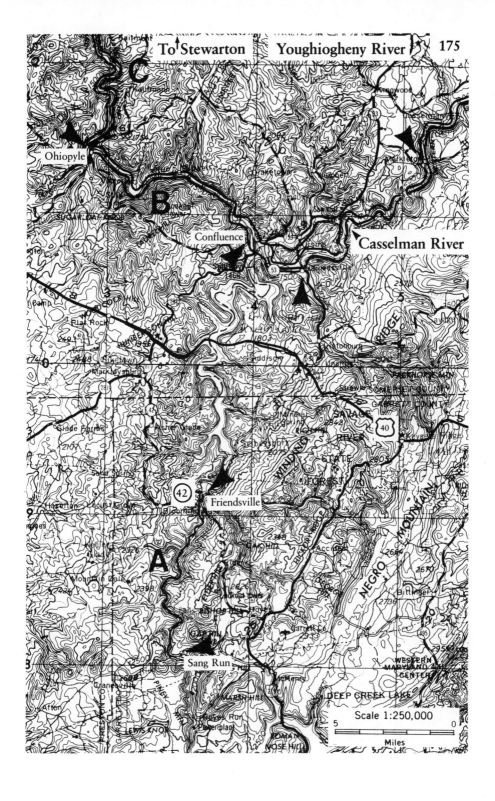

Casselman River

Scale 1:250,000

5   0

Miles

extremely sharp left-hand turn that must be made precisely to avoid running your boat several yards up on shore. Another vigorous but straightforward rock garden known as Dartmouth Slalom Rapids follows.

The final Loop rapids, Railroad, is another infamous boat chewer. Several passages exist over the steep drop, the most vigorous of which is slightly left of center, but you won't recognize it until you are right on it. If you wind up too far to the right you will be in a particularly juicy hydraulic known as Charlie's Washing Machine and it will be all over very quickly. A flip will take a boat or paddler a considerable distance in high water. Immediately after dropping over the ledge, you may have several options, depending on water level. If the water is low, you will have to immediately make a sharp left to avoid the next set of boulders. In high water, you can paddle straight ahead over them. If you've had enough, you can take out up a very steep bank on the right and take a long trail up to the picnic area.

Generally, paddlers spend a lot of time playing around on the Loop and then go on to Stewarton. For those not up on handling such rough water, a put-in can be made below Railroad Rapids and, with a few judicious carries, the trip can be made to Stewarton in comparative safety. The first 2 miles below the Loop are open and easily read Class 2 descents with only 1 dropping sharply.

Soon the river narrows and appears to end, but a loud roar coming from the left warns the paddler of a special treat. A paddler who is on this section for the first time may want to scout this—Dimple's Rapids— considered by some to be the most difficult of the lower Yough. The current is choked down into a bulging filament, smashes directly into a large boulder, and veers off to the right. Immediately below this is a dazzling combination of reefs and boulders, and below these are a long field of haystacks and a riverwide, gaping hydraulic (Swimmers' Rapids), followed by more haystacks; hence goofing Dimple's can make a long day for the paddler. Don't try to miss the big boulder at the top—ride right with the current and bounce off the pillow with the appropriate lean and brace.

Other gems before reaching the take-out are: Bottle of Wine, next below Swimmers; the Double Hydraulic, which is just what it says, and if you don't drive through the first, forget about the second; River's End, where huge boulders seemingly dam up the river but actually funnel it through a sharp left and steep drop; and Schoolhouse Rock, possibly so named because of the expensive tuitions it has collected in broached boats.

SHUTTLE: The Park Service has taken over shuttling, so you can just sit back and think about that day in the future when other rivers will be like the Yough. Tokens for the bus must be purchased at the put-in. Be sure to check for details as they may change after this writing.

GAUGE: At the put-in there is a boulder, which should be wet but not drowned. The gauge levels above are for the Confluence gauge available from the Pittsburgh National Weather Service, (412) 644-2890.

SAVAGE RIVER

Savage River Dam to Mouth at the North Branch — 5.5 Miles

CLASS	GRADIENT	VOLUME	SCENERY	TIME	LEVEL
	1@100				800–
2-4$_5$	63	S	A–B	1.5	1,400 cfs

MAPS: USGS—Westernport and Barton
Maryland state road map

DESCRIPTION: This is one of the more appropriately named rivers you will ever run. The Savage is small but fierce. It might be considered a 5.5-mile-long rapids, completely white except for 2 very small pools (1 just above the old Piedmont Dam, the other 400 yards from the mouth). The water is going downhill all of the way and is in a big hurry to get there. Running the river is dependent upon getting releases from the Savage River Dam through the cooperation of the Upper Potomac River Commission. Joe Monahan has popularized running this river and obtaining the releases. Generally the water is released for races at from 800 to 1,200 cfs, a lot of water for a stream you can almost spit across. Occasionally it is up in the winter months.

At 800 cfs, the water is mostly continuous Class 3. The waves are fairly high and little maneuvering is required. It is just one haystack after another, and it gives you the impression of riding a rocking horse instead of a whitewater craft.

At 1,200 cfs the river is something else. Most of the rocks are completely covered and well padded, but the force of the current and the power of the waves are greatly increased. The hydraulics are almost keeper-sized, and several waves are absolute stoppers. The paddler will find his attention glued to the action and many demands made on his paddling ability. The river is mainly Class 4 at this level due to the very continuous heavy water without let-up. Other than avoiding the larger holes, there is not much maneuvering required. Above 1,200 cfs the river can get very nasty and the hydraulics very dangerous. Consider this a 5.

DIFFICULTIES: The whole river. The chief difficulty is that there are hardly any rescue spots. Upon flipping, a hapless, boatless paddler can usually make it to shore in the narrow river without losing too much skin, but don't bet on it. It is extremely difficult to rescue the boat and other equipment, so the paddler should exert all effort to stay with his

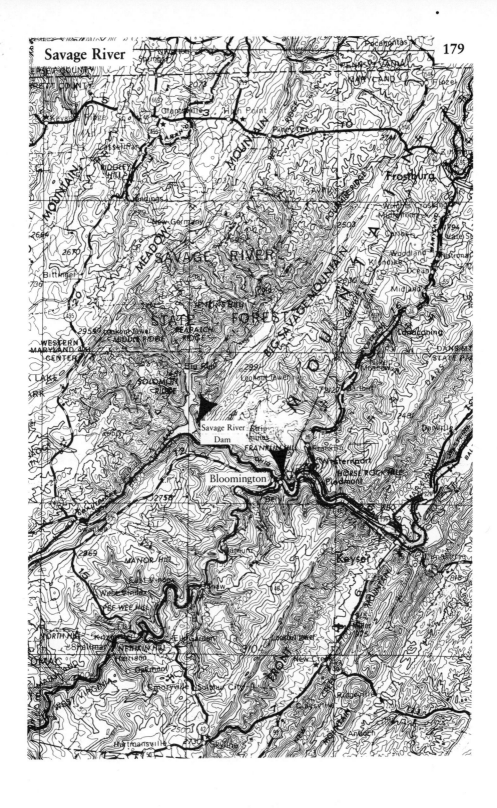

boat to help. There are no really dangerous spots until one reaches the old Piedmont Dam about a mile downstream from the first bridge. It is broken out on the left and can be run, but you tend to submarine into a mean hydraulic at 1,000 cfs or more. It is also broken out on the far right bank and is occasionally run there by the "suicide squad" types.

A half mile below the dam, the water becomes heavier and begins a steeper descent around a long right-hand bend where the river runs against the high roadbank. Where the river abruptly swings to the right leaving the road is a terrific drop through a heavy corkscrew set of violent waves called Criss-Cross opposite a boulder fittingly named Monument Rock. Below here are some mean hydraulics and a severe stopper, followed by a boulder on the left side of the river. Run this one as close to the right side of the boulder as possible, being careful not to get sucked into the vicious hole behind Memorial Rock on the right. At 1,200 cfs you can sneak to the left of the dry boulder. In this section the river is dropping the 100 fpm. It should be remembered that in addition to the hazards mentioned, there is also plenty of other continuously heavy whitewater.

One more warning. At every 1,200 cfs release, there always seems to be at least 1 or 2 jokers who think they can run this in an open boat. Usually the canoes look like some monster has chewed them up (which in fact it has) when they are salvaged after the water gets turned off. An *expert* can handle this solo in an open boat at 800 cfs, but he is very defensive about it. A pinned open boat is a hazard to navigation. Having to help rescue one is a hazard to life and limb.

SHUTTLE: The Savage River Road out of Bloomington, Maryland follows the river closely to the Savage River Dam and offers several steep put-in/take-out possibilities. To run all of the river, put in below the big dam (reached from a dirt road forking up on the river left just before the second bridge). At the end of the run, paddle up the North Branch to the bridge for a steep take-out. If in doubt as to whether you can handle the river, put in at the steel bridge 1 mile above the mouth. If you have trouble with this part (the easy portion), it wouldn't be advisable to run the rest.

GAUGE: Usually a timed release situation. If water is sufficient, there are usually at least 4 releases—late March, May, Labor Day weekend, and November. The middle 2 releases are for racing events and part of the river may be restricted for these purposes at such times. Heavy rains or snows permit additional releases.

CASSELMAN RIVER

Markleton to Harnedsville—11 Miles

CLASS	GRADIENT	VOLUME	SCENERY	TIME	LEVEL
1–3	25	649	A–B	4	2–4'

MAPS: USGS—Confluence 15'
      Pennsylvania state road map

DESCRIPTION: This is a very pleasant run for intermediates at medium water levels or for advanced paddlers at high water. It is up during most of the winter, and it comes up fast after rainy weather. This is an excellent second choice if you find the Yough too high. The water is acidic and polluted, but the action is pretty constant and varied. Many of the rapids in the upper part of the course are very long. However, you can usually find sneak routes if you prefer to avoid the big stuff. The lower course below Fort Hill becomes easier and interspaced with more flat water, but the scenery is good, giving way to more settled farmland. Most of the rapids occur at wide places in the river and many are straightforward, open descents. A few more are like larger rock gardens, but not requiring too much maneuvering, and there are only 2 or 3 potential trouble spots.

DIFFICULTIES: The rapids immediately after the easy opening rapids below the put-in bridge is a rather sharp left-hand turn. At the outside of the curve there is a large boulder always awash and creating a mean hydraulic downstream.

About 3 miles into the top run, the river appears to be dammed up by boulders. This is a complex drop and could be tricky to the inexperienced. Stay to the far left if in doubt, but remember that it will still be a double drop. In very high water, a girl scout route exists on the far right. At any level, the more entertaining descent is through the center and requires a sharp right-hand turn.

As you approach the second railroad bridge, avoid the extreme left as there are some keeper-sized hydraulics there in very high water. In low water, it is a sharp, dry drop.

There are no really difficult spots below Fort Hill unless you choose to make them so. About midway there is a nice rapids that turns sharply to the right against a fantastically beautiful waterfall entering the stream from the left. The river is divided by a large boulder at this point. An easy, but wavy run to the right, a very interesting fandango on the left!

SHUTTLE: The take-out is the bridge right below Harnedsville which is only 1 mile south of Confluence on PA 53. This road goes on out to US 40 only a few miles away. To reach the put-in, go north on PA 53 through Ursina and turn right. The river you cross is the Laurel Hill. In about 5 miles the first right takes you down to the midpoint for a short take-out at Fort Hill. The next right (4 more miles) takes you to Markleton.

GAUGE: The Markleton gauge is available via the National Weather Service in Pittsburgh, (412) 644-2890. No good riverside gauge except by inspection at take-out bridges (and this is reliable).

Index

Italic page numbers indicate maps.